Math, Programming, and Controllers

Ian Chow-Miller

Cavendish
Square

New York

Acknowledgments: The editors would like to thank John Long at Vassar College, Timothy Friez at Carnegie Mellon's Robotics Institute, Mishah U. Salman at Stevens Institute of Technology, and Suman Sabastin, a teacher in New York City, for their help in developing this series on robotics.

Published in 2017 by Cavendish Square Publishing, LLC
243 5th Avenue, Suite 136, New York, NY 10016

Cataloging-in-Publication Data

Names: Chow-Miller, Ian.
Title: Math, programming, and controllers / Ian Chow-Miller.
Description: New York : Cavendish Square Publishing, 2017. | Series: Robotics | Includes index.
Identifiers: ISBN 9781502619433 (library bound) | ISBN 9781502619440 (ebook)
Subjects: LCSH: Robots--Design and construction--Juvenile literature. | Robotics--Juvenile literature. |
LEGO Mindstorms toys--Juvenile literature.
Classification: LCC TJ211.2 C5345 2017 | DDC 629.8'92--dc23

Editorial Director: David McNamara
Editor: Fletcher Doyle
Copy Editor: Nathan Heidelberger
Associate Art Director: Amy Greenan
Designer: Alan Sliwinski
Production Coordinator: Karol Szymczuk
Photo Research: J8 Media

The photographs in this book are used by permission and through the courtesy of: Photo credits: Cover Produktionsbuero TINUS/Shutterstock.com; p. 4 Media for Medical/UIG/Getty Images; p. 7 Roslan Rahman/AFP/Getty Images; p. 14 Lucien Harriot/Getty Images; pp. 16, 18, 24, 31, 33, 42, 43, 47, 48, 65, 70, 72, 74, 76, 86, 95, 98, 101-103, 105-107, 109, 110 Ian Chow-Miller; p. 30 Courtesy VEX Robotics, Inc.; p. 34 Valerie Kuypers/AFP/Getty Images; p. 37 Courtesy Pitsco Education; p. 62 Chip Somodevilla/Getty Images; p. 68 Gisela Schober/Getty Images; p. 90 Chaikom/Shutterstock.com.

Printed in the United States of America

Contents

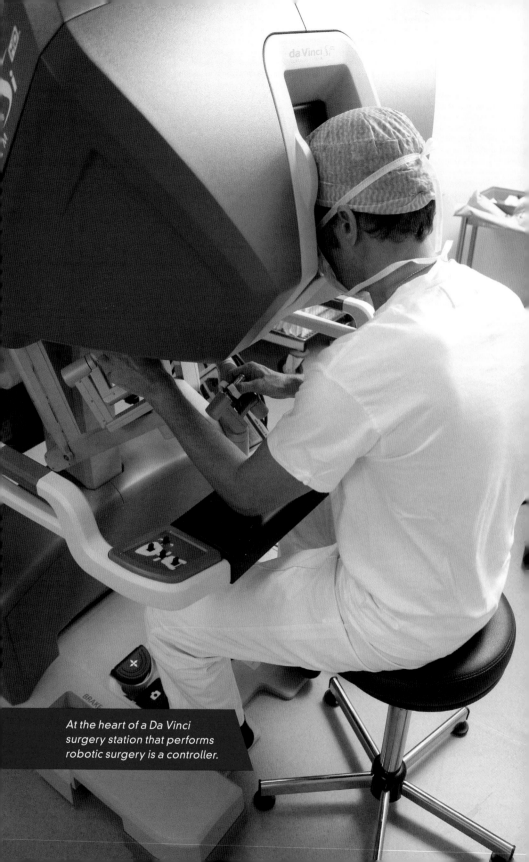

At the heart of a Da Vinci surgery station that performs robotic surgery is a controller.

1 Calling the Shots

When I run an introductory orientation for new sixth graders to my middle school, one of the fun games we play is called "Robot." I have students pair up and tell them to decide who has the longest hair. I then tell the student with the shortest hair that he or she is the **controller** and the one with the longest hair is going to be the robot. The controller will tap the robot on the head to make "it" go and to stop, will tap the right shoulder to make the robot turn right, and the left shoulder for a left turn. Then I let them begin and sit back with a smile. If you can picture 125 sixth graders walking around a gymnasium doing their best robot imitations while another 125 chase after them and try to give them **commands** to keep them moving while avoiding collisions with walls or other robots, then you can imagine the chaos that ensues.

In a very real sense, these "controllers" are behaving exactly the same way a robot controller behaves in the real world of robotics. By giving commands to their robots, they are controlling their actions. The game is an immense simplification of what most robot controllers are able to do, but at its core, the functions are the same. Give a command, robot responds, give another command, robot responds again. Don't give a command, robot continues following the last command and may walk into a wall or another student. (Often this is accomplished on purpose by a few cheeky controller-students.)

The world of robotics can become very complex. Robots may be taking in millions, even billions, of **bits** of information in seconds and reacting to that information in the blink of an eye. Take, for example, a self-driving car, like the ones that Google, Delphi, Mercedes-Benz, Nissan, and others are developing. They have to correlate GPS information with information from cameras, **distance sensors**, 360-degree **range-finding lasers**, **radar**, and other sources, and instantly calculate the best path to get you where you want to go without causing accidents or harm. At the basis of all this processing is the controller.

In a robot, a controller is a piece of **hardware** that will take in information and decide what to do with it; it is the hardware and **software** that in a very actual sense controls the robot. The controller can run automated (prewritten) programs. Within these programs, the controller can wait for information to come in from the **sensors** and make decisions based on that information by telling motors, lights, or other hardware attached to the robot to behave in a certain manner. Some controllers can store many programs, while some are very limited in storage space. Some controllers process information faster than others. And while some are capable of a dizzying array of actions, some can only complete a few basic ones.

A self-driving car uses a controller to read its many sensors and control its actions.

I purchased a BeeBot for my sons a few years ago. BeeBot is a little wheeled robot, with a yellow plastic shell that makes it look like a bee. It has buttons on it for *forward*, *backward*, *right*, *left*, *clear*, and *go* commands. These are the only commands it can carry out, and my sons have gleefully made obstacle courses on the kitchen floor out of cereal boxes and dinner plates so they can program BeeBot to drive from one end of the kitchen to another without crashing. As a way of contrast, the father of one of my students, who worked for Da Vinci Surgery, brought in one of its robots to show to my class a few years ago. The robotic surgery module came on a tractor-trailer and took several hours to set up in my classroom. At the heart of the robot was a set of "gloves" you placed your hands into, coupled with a pair of stationary "goggles" you looked through to see what you were doing. The screen you saw was a magnified practice field where you had to use little pincers attached to robotic arms to pick up tiny rubber bands (like the type used for dental braces) and hook them on wire loops about 0.5 inches (1.25 centimeters) in diameter. The pincers and the arms they were attached to were all controlled by the gloves you had slid your fingers and hands into. When you moved your head away from the goggles to see the actual size of the objects you were picking up, it was amazing. The computational processing power, sensory feedback, and motor control it took to coordinate all that movement was amazing. Yet at the heart of this surgical robot, and at the center of the BeeBot, was a controller.

From Simple to Complex

Controllers, as you can imagine, come in many styles, from the simple to the complex—those aimed at beginning robotics students to cutting-edge ones designed for industrial applications and everything in between. It should be noted that the term "controller" should not be confused with remote control. All robots have a controller. Some of these robots can be remote controlled. This simply means that the controller itself has the capability of taking in a signal remotely (without a wire attached) and acting upon it. The controller still has a preset program running which tells it how to respond to those signals; even when a robot is being moved by a "remote controller"—picture a large joystick with buttons on it—it is still the controller on the robot that is taking the information in and deciding what to do with it.

All information on a robot is digital. A wheel is turned because the motor it is attached to receives a digital signal in bits and **bytes** to allow a certain amount of voltage through, which in turn makes it spin for a set speed and time. Sensors send information into the controller in bits and bytes of data, indicating information about the world around them, which the controller then responds to based on its preset programs. So our controllers must be programmed to understand digital information, the endless stream of ones and zeros that cascade through it. They all do this with a **processor**.

If the controller is the brain of the robot, then the processor is the brain of the controller. The processor stores and executes programs; sends signals out to motors, lights, and other outputs; relays information; and receives information from the various sensors. The processor does the actual hardcore computing, the "processing" of signals and information, if you will. The other parts of the controller may consist of input and output **ports**; Wi-Fi, **Bluetooth**, or other remote signal receivers; a display screen; and interactive buttons for manually operating the controller. Not all controllers have these parts. It depends on the sophistication and intended use. For example, the **Arduino**, which has seen a quick rise to prominence in the **DIY** robotics community in the last five years, comes equipped with a processor, a serial connection port, fourteen digital input/output ports, six analog ports, a micro **USB** port, and a power port. While simple to use, the Arduino does take a bit of technical know-how, or at least the willingness to dive in and get your hands dirty figuring stuff out. A more out-of-the-box, ready-to-go controller would be the LEGO Mindstorms **EV3**. This controller (called "the **brick**") supplies the user with buttons to navigate a menu full of options, large file storage, a display screen, internal batteries, four output ports, four input ports, a USB port, a port for a Wi-Fi **dongle**, and even the ability to program the robot from the controller. The ports on the EV3 accept large **cables** with easy clip-in connectors that look similar to the old telephone jacks, while the Arduino accepts much smaller and more fragile **wires** known as pins. Each type of controller is suited to a specific use, and each will have its own advantages and disadvantages.

In this book, we will look at several different controllers, each serving a specific purpose. We will examine the EV3 brick and its close competitor, the VEX IQ. Both of these are designed for the middle-school classroom but have capabilities that far exceed their beginnings. The VEX IQ controller has built-in wireless programs that are ready to be operated by a purchasable joystick. The EV3 doesn't have a wireless remote control program that is pre-installed on the controller, but we will closely examine a way to write a program using Bluetooth communication, which can enable us to make a remote-controlled BattleBot with two EV3 brick controllers.

A note on the EV3 and VEX IQ nomenclature: The controllers themselves share the name with the larger robotics kit and (in the case of LEGO Education) the software they are sold with. I will use the terms interchangeably, such as EV3, EV3 brick, and EV3 controller.

We will examine several more advanced controller types, such as the VEX EDR, which takes the user to the next step by providing input and output ports and not much else, yet still is designed specifically for robotics applications. We will also look at how the famous **FIRST** Tech Challenge (**FTC**) robotics competition switched from the use of a ready-made controller (the LEGO NXT) to the use of two **Android phones** running MIT App Inventor. Before we move to totally DIY controllers which must be built and programmed from the ground up, such as the aforementioned Arduino, we will look at **shields** like Dexter Industries' **BrickPi**, which adapts the **Raspberry Pi** for use with LEGO NXT and EV3 motors and sensors. Finally we will see how the Arduino has become a game changer in the industry, allowing hobbyists and students to create totally customized and sophisticated robots without breaking the bank.

A controller is a powerful tool, but by itself it does not do much. It has the capability of communicating with the rest of your robot at speeds you can't imagine, and with a precision you can't accomplish on your own. But by itself, a controller is just a block of metal, plastic, and wires. You need to properly attach, wire, and program the controller in order for it to do anything. So along with our examination of different controllers, this book will cover attaching the controller to the robot, wiring a controller, and programming in both **graphical** and **text-based languages**. And we will discover that mathematic fundamentals like algebra and geometry lie at the heart of any good programming.

Programming Logic

At the middle school level, where I teach, as I introduce students to programming, they are often unaware of the math involved in the programming they are doing. For example, the classic line-following program using two light sensors is almost identical to the type of truth table students learn when studying logic and tautologies for the first time. You may have come across something like this in seventh-grade math:

A	B	A and B	A or B	Not A
False	False	False	False	True
False	True	False	True	True
True	False	False	True	False
True	True	True	True	False

We can program robots to follow a black line on a white surface using similar logic. By switching "true" and "false" to "senses black" and "senses white" and adding a column of robot actions such as "turn left," "turn right," "drive straight," and "stop," we can see how the process of a robot making decisions acts very similarly to the outcomes of a truth table. And it is, of course, the controller (specifically, its processor) that takes sensor information in and responds accordingly, doing this hundreds, even thousands, of times a second if it is programmed to (and fast enough—each processor is different).

But it is not simply in making logic-style decisions where math comes into play in robotics. Any good programmer will be able to incorporate math into his or her code. Coordination of robots moving synchronously can use algebraic functions to figure out the movements of each additional robot in a series. Robotics competitions will often have an item placed at a variable height on a pole. Our robot can use trigonometry to determine the height of the item and then retrieve it for points. Some of these examples and others will be elaborated upon in chapter three.

While the subjects covered in this book are supposed to be an introduction to the world of controllers, math, and programming, you may get overwhelmed, depending on your familiarity with the subjects. There is a glossary of common terms in the back of the book to help support your understanding of the subject. If at any time you feel like you're getting lost, go back to the example I began with. *Touch the top of the head*, move forward. *Touch it again*, stop. *Tap left shoulder*, turn left. *Tap right shoulder*, turn right. Try not to run into the wall or smash into another student's back. That's what a controller does. Communicate these movements without touching, and that's remote control. Add sophisticated movements (curved turn, pivot turn, point turn, specific degree turn), and you're programming at a higher level. Add some trigonometry to figure out the angle to turn based on the distance from two other objects, and you're ready to win!

Robots are built to help humans; this one picks up an unexploded bomb in New York City in September 2016.

2 Taking Control

Controllers can give us great flexibility when designing our robots, or they can limit us to a specific set of parts—usually those built by the same manufacturer. Some controllers allow almost any type of attachment, while others are so deeply integrated into the robot as to render their existence moot to the builder/programmer. Some controllers allow connections to an infinite variety of attachments using different protocols, while others, for the sake of simplicity (and to keep you buying the manufacturer's products), only allow you to connect with **proprietary** parts that have been designed to work with the controller.

In this chapter we will examine the breadth of controllers that you will typically find in a middle or high school robotics class; we will also look at those that are becoming standard in competitions like FIRST Tech Challenge. There are many to choose from, and as we go through them, hopefully you will be able to narrow down which one is the right one for you. There is no perfect controller; if there were, this book wouldn't be necessary. There is only the controller that fits your needs.

Whether you are building a robot to drive around your house and scare a cat, teaching a middle school class, preparing for a competition, or saving the world, the right controller is out there, and you should be able to identify it by the end of this book.

I am going to begin with an example of a robot that does not contain a controller we can do anything with other than simply program it. The BeeBot allows children as young as five to program it by pushing arrows and other command buttons like *pause*, *clear*, and *go*.

The BeeBot is a simple robot with a simple controller.

This simple robot will respond to whatever sequence of arrows are pushed. My kids could play with it for hours. And it does have a controller, only it's inside, and while there are colored shells you can add to BeeBot to decorate it, you can't take the yellow and black plastic shell off to get inside. This is intentional. The BeeBot is designed for kids and built with them in mind. No sensors or motors are attached externally, and no programming needs to be downloaded from an external source because it is all done "on board." Simply put, while there is a controller running this robot, it is not visible to us, and we cannot use it to modify the robot's function or purpose in any way. The point in writing about a controller that you can't actually access is to help illustrate that a controller does not have to be complex to meet the definition. The simplest robot will require some piece of hardware that helps to process commands and send them out to outputs like motors or speakers. Even a robot that doesn't move but just makes sounds and lights up has a controller. So while it does have an internal controller, if the BeeBot meets your needs as a builder/programmer then you can probably stop reading now. But it probably won't.

Moving Forward

The first actual controller we are going to look at is the new LEGO WEDO 2.0. While this is aimed at a younger crowd (second to fourth grade, according to LEGO Education) it is quite a bit more sophisticated than the BeeBot. The WEDO is the perhaps the simplest robotics set in which we would find something akin to a controller that we can use. Called the WEDO "**Smart Hub**," it connects to the computer or tablet via Bluetooth and has two slots for a combination of motors and/or sensors. The motors and sensors use the same proprietary connectors, which look like mini versions of a phone jack. You can program one motor and a sensor, or two sensors—the kits come with a tilt sensor and a motion sensor. You cannot, however, control two motors. The hub also does not have any interactive buttons other than the green on/off button you can see in the picture on page 18. Other than turning a program on, the Smart Hub has no interactivity—programs are started or stopped by pressing buttons on the device (tablet, laptop, or desktop). As we explore more controllers, we will discover this feature of the Smart Hub—only one interactive on/off button—means it has more in common with complex controllers than with some of the simpler ones.

The WEDO Smart Hub has a green on/off button and two ports.

While I call the WEDO 2.0 Smart Hub a simple controller, I don't want you to think it is weak or incapable of processing complex tasks. Complexity is a sliding scale when referring to programming and robots, but take a look at the following program written in the WEDO programming language.

WEDO allows you to create powerful programming with simple hardware.

By touching or clicking on the green arrow on the left side of this program, a set of commands will be sent to the WEDO robot. First it will turn on a motor clockwise at power level 8 for 4 seconds. Next a "boing" sound will play. (Each sound has a preset number. In this case, number 6 is a "boing!") After the sound, the hub itself will flash purple (preset color number 2) and will repeat this action four times. In the last bit of programming, the motor will turn on counterclockwise until the tilt sensor is tilted "up," at which point the motor will stop. That's a relatively short and simple program. The hub may not be an Arduino Uno, but it can do a fair bit.

The LEGO WEDO 2.0 "Smart Hub" is a controller. It is not a very advanced or sophisticated one, but it does serve as the hardware piece that executes programs by processing information, sending signals to motors, and reading information from sensors. And that is as good a definition as any for us to use as we being to examine some of the more advanced and sophisticated controllers available to use.

Common Controllers

The next two controllers we are going to examine fall into a unique category: they are sophisticated in the sense that they have powerful processors and can interact with many motors and sensors, while at the same time they work best mainly with a proprietary set of input and output devices and are designed to do things a specific way rather than allowing the user to configure things in their own way. For example, they both have internal speakers, rather than allowing a user to wire in a speaker of their own choice. And while one of them is open source in both hardware and software, they both work best when using parts and languages developed by the company that makes the controllers themselves. I am referring to the LEGO Mindstorms Education EV3 (EV3 from here on out) and the VEX Robotics IQ (VEX IQ).

The EV3 and IQ are phenomenal controllers. Using them in my classes, my students have created amazing drag racers, search-and-rescue robots, candy-sorting factories, BattleBots, and others. They have programmed robots that can navigate mazes, throw projectiles at targets, play songs, and dance with other robots. The reason they are such good controllers is that they are part of a robotics kit. In the words of LEGO Education, they are a "solution" that has been developed and refined over many years to meet the needs of middle school classrooms. They come with everything you need—a developed software environment, easily attachable motors and sensors— and they are easy to **prototype** with modular building pieces. In the case of LEGO, these are pieces that generations of children have played with for more than sixty years. These factors and many more make these controllers the top choice of many educators and hobbyists. Let's take a look at the two more closely.

Both the EV3 and IQ controllers come with an internal power source—a rechargeable lithium ion battery. The battery snaps or slides into the underside of each controller, actually forming part of the body of the controller but also making them a bit bulky because of the integrated battery. Both have an **LCD** screen for things like display of program names, battery charge, sensor and motor readings, displaying words and/or pictures in programs, configuring Bluetooth connections, and other useful information. The EV3 controller (referred to by LEGO as the "brick") has a USB slot for a Wi-Fi dongle and a **micro SD card** slot for expanding memory power when recording science experiments.

The similarities don't stop there. Both controllers have connection points for motors and sensors. These ports accept cables with a jack similar to a phone jack. And here is where we begin to see some of what is limiting these products from being world class and able to be utilized in professional and industrial situations. For while their sensors are powerful, and while, in the case of EV3, there are companies that make **third-party** sensors for the brick, all the sensors must attach using cables with these proprietary jacks. As we will see later on in this chapter, high-end controllers are built to accept industry-standard sensors that utilize similar protocols such as **I2C** and **analog** and **digital sensors**, as well as **DC** and **servo** (both standard and continuous rotation) **motor** controller ports. All these allow for a far greater range of sensors, motors, and other attachments than either the EV3 or the VEX IQ.

On the EV3, there are four motor ports labeled A through D, and four sensor ports labeled 1 through 4. VEX IQ has done something different and added twelve ports that it calls "smart ports" because each port can accept either a motor or a sensor. This adds a small but significant advantage over the EV3 in that you don't have to worry as much about cables reaching your controller as you're building your robot. Another difference is that the EV3 is "open source," meaning the documentation on all its software and hardware is available for anyone to look at. This is why there are more third-party sensors for the EV3 than for VEX IQ. You can also use (with some modification) older LEGO parts like the NXT motors and sensors with EV3. To pair with these controllers, both companies produce a type of touch sensor, distance sensor, gyro sensor, and color sensor. While these differ in several aspects, they form the core of what both of these controllers work with.

Remote Control

One final aspect of these two controllers I would like to cover before we move on: remote control. We have to discuss how we can control these robots remotely. In the case of VEX IQ, there is a radio attachment you can add to your controller to pair with a remote control similar to a game controller for popular video games.

You can write your own program, mapping each move on the game controller to a signal given to any of the VEX IQ smart ports to execute, or you can use the built-in commands the way they come. With the EV3, there are a few options for remote control. There is an app called Robot Commander made by LEGO that controls EV3 robots built in standard configurations via Bluetooth. There is also an infrared remote called the IR Beacon and an infrared sensor that come standard with the home (as opposed to education) version of the EV3 kit. When the sensor is attached to the controller, it can determine which buttons are being pushed on the IR Beacon and respond accordingly. However, my favorite way to remotely control an EV3 is by using the internal Bluetooth capabilities and creating a remote control by using one EV3 controller to control another robot. This is part of my end-of-course unit in robotics. I have each pair of students with a robot team up with another pair, forming a group of four with two controllers. Their job is to build and program a remote-controlled BattleBot using their two controllers and Bluetooth communication. As you can imagine, this is also one of my students' favorite units. In chapter five, I will go over in detail how to remotely control one EV3 controller with another.

Both the EV3 and VEX IQ are integral parts of fully realized robotics systems that you can do amazing things with. However, they both have limitations discussed in the previous paragraphs, mainly that they only interface with their own hardware or third-party hardware designed to go with that particular controller. That's not realistic in the business world. Imagine if you are a company that makes a line of robotics sensors. In order to increase your market share, you want to make sensors that are not only of exceptional quality but are also able to be used with as many controllers as possible. If you are limited to one particular controller, then your success depends on the popularity of that one controller, no matter how good the quality of your sensors are. So as we move up the ladder toward more and more sophisticated controllers, one of the important rungs on that ladder will be the ability for a controller to interface with hardware built by any vendor.

The VEX Cortex, which is part of their EDR line, bridges the gap between controllers that are designed for specific sensors and those that are totally open to any sensor that meets standard protocols. The VEX Cortex will also allow us to learn about and understand what some of those protocols are. Visible in the Cortex below are a series of open ports for sensors and motors to plug into. On first inspection they all look similar, but upon closer inspection they are labeled differently, and each type will only accept specific parts. To begin with, you'll notice that the motor on the right has two wires, black and red. The light sensor on the left has three wires, black, red, and yellow. The placement of the motor is important because while the VEX Cortex has ten motor slots, only two of them, number one and number ten, accept two-wire motors. The rest of the slots are for three-wire motors.

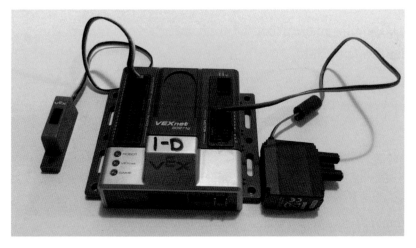

The VEX EDR Cortex with a motor (right) and a light sensor (left). I2C ports are top right.

Down to the Wire

The wires on most sensors and motors are important and mean different things. So let's take a look at that two-wire motor, called the VEX 393 motor. VEX used to make all of its motors three-wire. A typical three-wire motor would have one wire (almost always black) be the **ground**, the red wire the voltage, and the yellow wire would be something that handles the pulse width modulation (**PWM**). PWM is a method for controlling the speed on most DC (direct current) motors. Let me illustrate this concept with an example. If the maximum voltage on a motor is given at 10 **volts**, then full speed for that motor would be 10 volts and half speed would be 5 volts. This causes some problems because you would have to constantly drop the voltage to go slower, which also means that you are decreasing the **torque** (rotational strength) of your motors by only running at half power. This could cause **stalling** at slower speeds for two-wire motors—sometimes there simply would not be enough power to get them going at slower speeds. So a third wire was added to allow for PWM on motors.

When using PWM, motors are constantly on at full voltage, 10 volts in our example. The voltage would actually pulse, on and off, 10 and 0 volts. This pulsing of voltage would occur thousands of times per second, way too fast for humans to notice while watching our robots move. If you wanted your robot to go forward at half speed, instead of dropping to 5 volts, you would have an equal number of on and off voltage. If you average 10 and 0, you have 5 volts, which would give our robot half speed but still full power because our voltage would still be at a full 10 volts. If you want your robot to go a little faster, let's say at 75 percent of full speed, you would increase the length of time for each pulse, the pulse width. This ratio between the on and off times is called the duty cycle. The time that the pulse is off for does not change, but the time that it is on for does. So by increasing the pulse width (the actual amount of time the voltage is on for) you increase the duty cycle and the speed of the motors. To reduce the speed, you would shorten the pulse width, which decreases the duty cycle and slows your motors.

Wait! This discussion was about the VEX two-wire 393 motors. They only have a ground and a voltage wire, no PWM wire. Why is that? To control the speed, VEX added an **H-bridge**. An H-bridge is a device that controls the speed of the motors. There is one attached to motor port ten and one attached to motor port one on the VEX Cortex. So what is the point of all this? Well, you can only use VEX two-wire motors in ports one and ten of a VEX Cortex controller, but you can use any standard DC three-wire motor (designed to be used with a maximum of 7.2 volts) with ports two through nine. This having been said, you should definitely test any non-VEX motors that you are attaching to the Cortex to make sure they are compatible and work at the speeds and power you want.

A closer look at the Cortex will help us understand some of the other standard protocols for robotics controllers:

We're already familiar with the motors, and you can see the VEX two-wire 393 motor plugged into port one in the image on page 24. Above that is another set of ports labeled UART1, UART2, and I2C. This is another case where the Cortex can work with non-VEX devices, as I2C is one of those standard protocols I mentioned earlier. I2C stands for "Inter-Integrated Circuits." An I2C device is a **bus** used to coordinate and communicate between several devices, such as sensors, and a main controller. In the world of electronics, a bus is a system that helps parts communicate with each other in a computer or controller. A bus refers to the hardware, wires, and other parts that accomplish this. The Cortex allows any bus that is using I2C protocol to communicate with it. This can allow for dozens of sensors to work with your robot.

In the Cortex, as in almost all the devices we have looked at, there will be a ground wire. The pin for this goes into the hole closest to the characters "I2C" where they are written on the Cortex. Working from there we have a hole for the pin connected to a 5-volt wire. This is an optional wire as not all devices you are communicating with over your I2C bus will require extra supplied voltage. The next two pinholes are the most important. The third one is for the wire called the serial clock line (**SCL**). The SCL synchronizes the messages coming in from all the devices connected through the I2C bus. The maximum number of possible devices is more than one hundred, more than you can use. Finally, the last wire to connect to the Cortex is the **SDA**, or serial data line. This is where the information, in bits and bytes, is communicated between the controller and the bus. With thousands of messages from multiple sources whooshing back and forth at speeds of several thousand bytes per second, you can see how important that SCL line is for keeping all those messages out of each others' way.

That is a lot of information for a single port on a **microcontroller**. But you can imagine how this one little port can expand your Cortex beyond connecting with a few of VEX's proprietary sensors to communicating with tons of third-party sensors. The **UART** protocol doesn't allow for communication with dozens of devices, but it does allow some very specific actions that could not be achieved with the other protocols.

Video Display

UART stands for "universal asynchronous receiver/transmitter." It can both receive and send information. The most common UART devices are LCD display screens. The VEX IQ and EV3 have integrated LCD display screens, but most controllers, including the VEX Cortex, do not come similarly equipped. In this case, VEX has made an LCD display device to connect to your Cortex. The back of the LCD module has two ports, one for data out and one for data in. A four-wire Y serial cable connects these two ports. "Serial" in this case means data moves in one direction; the Y refers to a split in the wire that allows one top of the "Y" to connect to the data-in port while the other end connects to the data-out port. These two separate ends eventually come together into a four-wire end at the base of the "Y" that can then be plugged into the Cortex. One wire is ground, one is for voltage (5V), one is for data in, and one is for data out. The reason there are separate wires for data is because there is nothing similar to the SCL protocol in I2C that can control and line up the information. It is, after all, asynchronous.

Theoretically you can connect any UART devices to the UART ports on the Cortex, but in reality it would be quite hard. For any device you connect that is not proprietary (not made by the company that makes the controller), you have to configure the software to accept it. In some cases, like third-party analog sensors, this is quite easy; in others, like UART, it could get messy.

The last two sections of the VEX Cortex are reserved for sensors. There are ports for digital sensors, analog sensors, and one port for a speaker—this is located at the bottom of all the digital ports. From left to right, the three pinholes on the sensor ports are for the ground wire, 5V wire, and signal wire. The signal wire will send the signal, in bits and bytes, back to the Cortex. Digital sensors are ones that will return a specific state in discreet values: 1, 2, 3, 4, 5, for example. The classic example of a digital sensor in this case would be a touch sensor: 1 for on or pushed in, 0 for not on or pushed in. An analog sensor is going to deliver a range of values—for example, a light sensor that returns values from 1 to 1,500 based on what it is sensing. The digital sensor converts its data to the preset values; the analog shows us more raw data. The sensor ports are the part of this controller where accepting third-party products is going to be the easiest. As long as the sensor is a three-wire sensor (ground, 5V, signal), it should be compatible.

DETERMINING VALUES

An object 20 centimeters (8 inches) away from another object may read as 50 centimeters (20 inches) if you are using a nonproprietary sensor. Using the **debugging** and sensor reading features of most software programs like ROBOTC, you need to see what values your robot is returning and write a simple line of math code to adjust those values so they work for you.

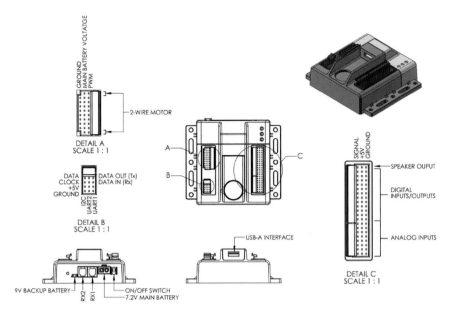

GROUND
MAIN BATTERY VOLTAGE
PWM

2-WIRE MOTOR

DETAIL A
SCALE 1 : 1

A

C

SIGNAL
+5V
GROUND

SPEAKER OUPUT

DATA
CLOCK
+5V
GROUND

DATA OUT (Tx)
DATA IN (Rx)

B

DIGITAL
INPUTS/OUTPUTS

I2C
UART2
UART1

DETAIL B
SCALE 1 : 1

USB-A INTERFACE

ANALOG INPUTS

DETAIL C
SCALE 1 : 1

9V BACKUP BATTERY

RX2
RX1

ON/OFF SWITCH
7.2V MAIN BATTERY

This diagram from VEX shows all of the ports in its controller.

Just because a sensor is compatible does not mean it is going to work right away or smoothly integrate with the Cortex and the software you are using to control it. If you use a different distance sensor from VEX's standard **ultrasonic range finder**, it should work well enough with the Cortex, but you may have to adjust the values you are receiving so they make sense for you.

If you are using a sensor that is totally alien to the Cortex, you may run into some trouble. First of all, the sensor must be three-wire. You may have to write new drivers (code supplied to the cortex) for the cortex to recognize and work with it. You may want to plug it in and tell the software it is a different sensor. You may be able to get readings that can be used. Remember, the Cortex has no idea what is being plugged into it. It only knows that one pin is ground, one is voltage, and one is a signal.

Building on a Breadboard

There are two controllers that fit into interesting categories that are not easily defined but distinguish themselves from all the others. The first of these is the BoeBot Basic Stamp. The Board of Education (BOE) Basic Stamp is a microcontroller that is sold as part of a kit to help students understand what happens "under the hood" of a robot like an EV3 or NXT. The emphasis on these robots is on the wiring and circuitry on the board.

The actual controller (microcontroller in this case) is the Stamp, which in the picture below is located on the bottom-left quadrant on the board, to the left of the on/off switch. I have placed two resistors in the white plastic **breadboard** on the right side of the board. All the attachments to the BOE board are made using input and output (I/O) pins connected to this breadboard, including the servo motors that power the BoeBot.

The Basic Stamp is a tool for teaching wiring and circuitry.

This type of connection is meant to teach the user how signals are sent through electronic circuitry to make a robot work. This is a worthwhile endeavor, but beyond that, the capabilities of this board and microcontroller are limited.

The other type of controller that I want to mention is called a shield. A shield is a piece of circuitry created to fit over an existing controller or existing circuitry to expand the capabilities of that circuitry. The BrickPi by Dexter Industries is a shield that converts a Raspberry Pi into a robot that is compatible with LEGO NXT and EV3 motors and sensors. Raspberry Pi is a relatively new product that has revolutionized microcomputing in a short period. Basically a circuit board with attachments for micro-USB, power, monitors, ethernet, and other basic computer **peripherals**, it runs on its own operating system that can be booted from an SD card. The Raspberry Pi is not very useful as a robotics controller. It is designed to be a computer. When you add the shield provided by Dexter Industries, you have created a robot that can run NXT and EV3 motors and sensors but also has Wi-Fi and networking capabilities.

Versatile Performers

This chapter has covered controllers that are limited in what they can do as well as ones that allow us a great deal of flexibility. I want to look at one last controller, one that is perhaps the top choice for hobbyists who want an easy-to-use controller that allows them to attach any peripheral: the Arduino.

The Arduino is the name of a suite of controllers, like the Arduino Uno, the Mega, the Zero, the 101, and so forth. They differ in shape and size and in the number and type

The UNO is among the suite of controllers made by Arduino.

of connections they have. Let's look at the Arduino Uno as an example.

The Arduino has a USB port and a jack for AC power. It accepts digital PWM, which allows control of motors and other devices. There are analog and digital inputs for sensors as well. This Arduino comes with 32KB of flash memory, enough to store any program you can write for it. All Arduino controllers are programmed using the Arduino IDE (Integrated Development Environment). This software is open source. There is plenty of documentation and sample programs for it on the internet.

The Arduino Uno is popular due to its low price point, its ease of use, its open-source software, and the lack of any soldering to connect circuits. In the next chapter, we will look at two more controllers, the Tetrix Prizm, and the suite of Modern Robotics controllers that are used in the FIRST Tech Challenge competition.

Students work togethers to control their creations at a FIRST Tech Challenge.

3 Finding the Right One

U nderstanding controllers and choosing the right one for your desired use is no easy task. Hopefully the last two chapters have provided you with the basic understanding of what controllers can do and of which one might be the right one for you to use for a specific application. I am going to look at two more controllers in this chapter, ones that meet the advanced needs of students who are first branching out into the world of robotics beyond what EV3 and VEX IQ have to offer. These controllers are the Tetrix Prizm and the setup used to run the new FIRST Tech Challenge robots. The controller in this latter case is actually a smart phone running an Android OS. After we finish our examinations of these two controllers, this chapter will finish with a look at how to program them and how mathematics applies to our programming world. Let's first take a look at the Prizm.

I was excited as a teacher when I saw the Prizm in the new Tetrix catalog as it really seems to hit a target market of young high school students who want to have total control and flexibility in making their robots, while staying away from industry-level computing and electronics. The Prizm looks cool. It has a clear **polycarbonate** case, so it is strong. This is one controller whose case is clearly not going to break easily. The Prizm itself is built upon Arduino architecture. Similar to how the shield built by Dexter Industries attaches to make the BrickPi robot, the Prizm is built on top of Arduino hardware. But instead of using socket pin connections like the Arduino does, the Prizm allows us to connect to standard three- and four-pin sensors and motors. And the Prizm is not just an addition to the Arduino the way the BrickPi is to the Raspberry Pi; it is a fully integrated board. Let's take a look and examine it a bit more closely.

I'm going to start in the bottom left corner with the red stop/reset button and go counterclockwise from there. This button clearly is to stop programs from running and to reset the robot so it is ready for the next signal. Next to that is a start button, and while this should be self-explanatory, it should be noted that the inclusion of these two buttons with no others indicates the robot stores and runs one program at a time. This distinguishes it from a younger student model like the EV3, where you can store many programs on the brick. Sometimes I have students who have to scroll through thirty or more program names to find the one they want.

The two DC motor control ports with the black (-) and red (+) ports here are designed to accept **Anderson Powerpole connectors**. These connectors have become the de facto standard in electrical transmission of high DC currents in robotics and other applications. The connectors became really popular because they are easy to use, easy to adapt existing

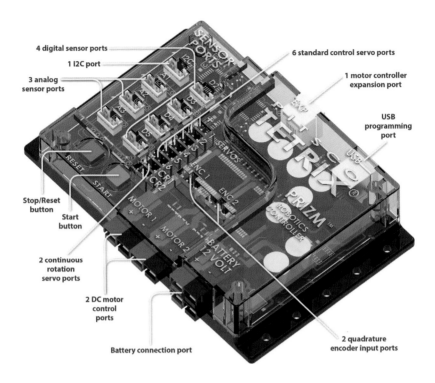

4 digital sensor ports

1 I2C port

3 analog
sensor ports

6 standard control servo ports

1 motor controller
expansion port

USB
programming
port

Stop/Reset
button

Start
button

2 continuous
rotation
servo ports

2 DC motor
control
ports

Battery connection port

2 quadrature
encoder input ports

The new Tetrix Prizm has a polycarbonate case to provide protection.

wires with older connectors, and much less likely to loosen, break, or rip apart. Often, especially with robots designed by inexperienced students, the connection between the wire coming from a DC motor and the motor ports on a controller would come apart. This could be really frustrating when you have built a great robot, written a robust program, and are in the middle of a competition, only to find that a motor stops working because of a small connector. The Anderson Powerpole connectors (other similar ones are now made by other companies) have reduced, though certainly not eliminated, this problem.

To the right of the DC motor control ports, you see similar connectors for a 12V DC battery, which is standard for most Tetrix products. Though there are two sets of connectors and you can use the top or bottom to wire in your battery, you may not use both to wire in two sets of 12V DC batteries. This very well could fry your circuits, and that would not be a good thing. The second set of connectors is to wire power out if you are adding on hardware—for example, another motor controller. Tetrix says it is producing expansion items just like this to work with the Prizm very soon.

Above the DC motor controller ports you'll find two encoder ports (labeled ENC1 and ENC2). These are designed for **quadrature encoders**, which are sensors that attach to DC motors and can measure position and location of a rotating motor. Though there are different types, most often a quadrature encoder uses an optical sensor to "see" the rotation of a shaft. Attached to the shaft in a circular fashion will be two sets of alternating black and white colors. These are out of phase with each other so that if black on the first wheel is followed by white on the second wheel, the sensor knows the motor is rotating in one direction, and vice versa. The colors are evenly spaced so that the sensor can determine speed based on how often the black and white pulses go by the optical sensor.

As we work our way around the board, you'll notice the USB connection; this uses the USB A to B protocol, and while this particular type of USB cord is not as common as it used to be, the Prizm does ship with one. Next to the USB port is a motor controller expansion port. This is where you would wire in the aforementioned expansion DC motor controller. The connection seems to utilize a standard ethernet cable connection.

Coming back to the center of the Prizm, there are three rows of ports. The first of these, above the green start button, are servo motor ports. The first six on the top are traditional servo motor ports, while the bottom two are for continuous rotation servos. Whereas a DC motor has two wires and is controlled by the amount of power sent to it via pulse width modulation, a servo motor contains a DC motor inside, along with internal gears and a shaft encoder for exact positioning. Servo motors contain three wires, one for voltage, one for ground, and one for signal. For a more complete description of the difference between servo and DC motors, please see *Integrated Robotics*, another volume in this series.

Finally, there are two rows of sensor ports. There are four digital sensor ports, and all the way on the left-hand end are four analog sensor ports. The top port in the analog row is an I2C port, while the top digital sensor port can also be configured as a serial port.

The Prizm is "**plug and play**," with all the ports ready to accept motors (DC and servo) and sensors (analog and digital) made by Tetrix. But because the ports are all standard, there is no reason why the ports cannot accept third-party hardware quite easily. For example, there is no reason the DC motor ports should not accept another 12V DC motor. A DC motor is going to be two-wire, and if you connect the two wires (positive and ground) to an Anderson Powerpole connector, it should plug right in and work without any trouble. The quadrature encoder ports may be a bigger problem because the quadrature motor encoders designed by Tetrix are manufactured to pair with their motors. That said, if you purchase another company's DC motors, there is no reason not to purchase encoders to match as well.

Similar considerations are to be taken with the sensors and motors. An analog sensor and a digital sensor both send a specific type of information: either discreet numbers (digital) or a range of values (analog). The Prizm has the added advantage of using the Arduino software (IDE), which makes it easy to configure any type of sensor you want. Since the Arduino is open source, there is a ton of information available on the internet to show you how to make the Prizm user friendly for whatever hardware you're using with it.

Ease of Use

We ended the last chapter with a look at the Arduino Uno and began this chapter with a controller that is built around the Arduino. However, I would say that the Prizm is more than just the shield the BrickPi is. So what's the difference? Can you do everything with the Arduino Uno that you can with the Prizm? Yes, you can. The major difference is ease of use. The Arduino accepts socket pins, which means most of your devices will have to be mounted to a breadboard of some type in order to make them fully functional because, as we know, our power, sensors, and motors require more than a single socket pin to function. They usually involve two-, three-, or four-wire components. The Arduino does have the advantage of teaching you what it takes to put a full circuit together. If you are successful with what you build with an Arduino, you can take the next step and etch a PCB circuit board and solder on all your components. This is robotics at its most fundamental level. But the focus of this book is for the high school student or competitor, and while the Arduino is a great controller for prototyping, a board like the Prizm offers a great deal of flexibility and functionality while having the plug-and-play features that allow the user to prototype quickly and make changes without moving a bunch of socket pins around a breadboard.

Each controller we have looked at so far has been a fully integrated approach to robotics. Whether it was a simple WEDO Smart Hub, a microcontroller like the Arduino, or an advanced controller built for use with specific parts like the VEX Cortex, each of these is an individual device. The next (and last) controller we are going to examine is different from all others. That's because this controller is actually an Android phone, or one using the Android operating system. Specifically, one of the following is allowed: a ZTE Speed, Motorola Moto G second or third generation, Google Nexus, or Samsung Galaxy S5. These phones are chosen because they run on the Android operating system, are relatively easy to download the software onto, and can communicate with each other easily via built-in wireless radio.

I know what you're thinking. How on earth do you connect motors and sensors and 12-volt battery packs to a phone? The answer is you don't. While the phone is referred to in the competition as the "Robot Controller," it is obviously different from every other controller we have looked at so far. First of all, the phone must be paired with a second one of the same

FEELING WIRED

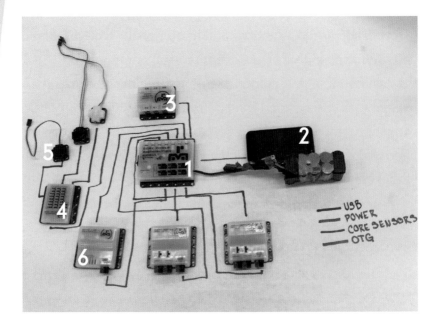

Above is a basic wiring diagram for all of the major FTC components as set up by members on my team. The Core Power Distribution Module (CPDM) in the center (1) of the picture is the one that connects to all the others. It connects to the phone, the battery, and all the other device interface modules (2). Directly on top of the CPDM is the Core Legacy Module (3). This module is designed to work with legacy NXT sensors. (Until 2015, FTC used the LEGO NXT as its controller, and that allowed NXT sensors as well.) The Legacy Module connects to the CPDM via USB only. The phone on the right connects via a USB **OTG cable**. OTG (on-the-go) is a protocol that allows a USB device to be both a slave and a master. To the left of the CPDM is a Core Device Interface Module (4). This connects most three-pin digital and analog sensors. You'll notice the three sensors depicted here (5, *from left*: IR Seeker,

Optical Distance Sensor, and Touch Sensor) connect using the yellow, red, and black three-wire protocol we discussed in the last chapter. This device interface also only needs a USB connection to the main module. The bottom three modules (6) all connect to the CPDM with both power and USB. The one on the left is a servo controller, and the two on the right are both DC motor controllers.

The photo below shows what all of these modules look like connected to sensors and motors. And if that looks like a mess, imagine what it looks like on a robot! In the next chapter on troubleshooting, I'll include a section on cable management.

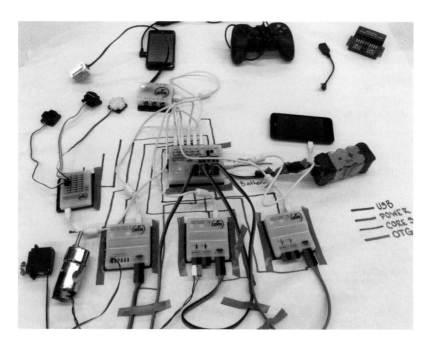

make and manufacture. One phone is held by the driver during competition. This phone can operate as both a starter device for autonomous actions (the robot moves on its own as determined by a preset program) and as a remote for the driver during the driver-controlled portion of the competition. Not that the driver actually uses the phone to control the robot. The driver, or drivers, connects game pads to the phone via USB to operate the drive and other motors on the robot.

If you're following so far, you've got one phone at the drivers' base with one or two game controllers connected to it. That phone is connected to another one, the "Robot Controller," which is mounted on the actual robot. And it is this second phone that sends information to the motors and reads and processes information from the sensors. It is, of course, connected to all those modules.

Programming

Programming all of these controllers requires a special set of skills that are luckily easier to master today than they've ever been. That is due to several factors. To begin with, coding programs like the Hour of Code and Scratch have brought the basics to kids as young as five or six. My kindergarten-aged son spent two hours on his device playing with the Scratch Jr. app while he was bored at his older brother's tae kwon do competition. Once you reach the upper elementary grades, you have programs like WEDO, which is a totally graphical programming environment, and EV3, which is a very powerful graphical programming language. And if you are comfortable with graphical programming environments but want to learn more, you can write a program in ROBOTC for VEX graphical and then convert it to text with the click of a button.

With these tools, it is easier than ever to learn programming, and no matter what the language you are using is, the fundamentals still apply: loops, *if/then* statements, **functions**, and naming of motors and sensors. And whatever the programming language, robots do not think, they just obey commands in the order you tell them to, whether or not the commands or results make sense to a human. While being easier than ever to learn, the plethora of languages for robots leads to a small problem. There are too many programming languages to cover them all and provide examples in this book. Instead, I am going to focus on ROBOTC because it comes in many versions. It can be used to run VEX IQ and Cortex, LEGO Mindstorms NXT and EV3, and there are even several versions of ROBOTC that can be used to run different Arduino controllers.

This programming section will show you how to achieve basic and complex behaviors with your robot. It will also cover some situations where we can apply mathematical principles to our programming in order to make it more robust or help it solve a particularly sticky problem. To begin with, almost all robots need to be configured in the software. This means that the software needs to know where we have connected motors and sensors, and what kind of sensors there are.

Setting Things Up

We will use ROBOTC as our first example of how to configure your robot. In ROBOTC, there are two ways to accomplish this. You can write the code yourself, or you can generate it using a setup tool. Due to the complexity of syntax involved (one wrong character typed and your robot will try to communicate with a motor in a sensor port), I prefer to use the setup tool. In ROBOTC, this is called "Motors and Sensors Setup."

When you click Motors and Sensors Setup, a window will open that allows you to configure different motors and sensors on the VEX Cortex. In the next chapter, I will show you how to work with the ROBOTC code to accept a third-party sensor that is not automatically available in the set-up configuration.

Once you open the configuration tool, you will see several tabs across the top: one for motors, one for analog sensors, and one for digital sensors. Let's start with the motors first.

The Motors tab allows us to configure different styles of motors and name them. When you name a motor or sensor, call it something simple that makes sense for what you will use it for or as. Sometimes students have a habit of getting a little wacky with their nomenclature, and while that can be fun at first, it often leads to confusion later on.

In the example on page 47, I have named my motors *rightMotor*, *leftMotor*, and *armMotor* because that is what they will be used for. Notice that I left the first word with a lowercase first letter and the second word with an uppercase first letter (and no space between them). This is standard syntax for programming. Since my right and left motors are

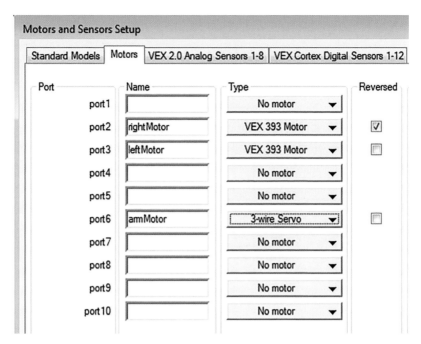

Motors and Sensors Setup

| Standard Models | Motors | VEX 2.0 Analog Sensors 1-8 | VEX Cortex Digital Sensors 1-12 |

Port	Name	Type	Reversed
port1		No motor ▼	
port2	rightMotor	VEX 393 Motor ▼	☑
port3	leftMotor	VEX 393 Motor ▼	☐
port4		No motor ▼	
port5		No motor ▼	
port6	armMotor	3-wire Servo ▼	☐
port7		No motor ▼	
port8		No motor ▼	
port9		No motor ▼	
port10		No motor ▼	

Use the Motors tab to configure your motors, and name them. Match the motor names to the functions they will perform.

my drive motors, they are going to be DC motors (VEX 393 by name), and the arm motor is a three-wire servo. You'll also notice that to the right of port 2 there is a column titled "Reversed" that is checked off. This is a classic setup for a two-motor drivetrain—a robot where there is one drive motor on either side. If you hold two motors facing the same way, then a command to turn them on will send them both turning the same way. If you now take one of those motors and flip it around so it is turned 180 degrees from the first motor, it looks the same, but that same command to move forward will actually have the flipped motor spinning in the opposite direction. The "Reversed" command counteracts this by assuming all instructions to that motor should be turned in the opposite direction. For example, if you entered a command *setMotor(rightMotor, 50)*; *setMotor(leftMotor,50)*, it would turn on both motors in a direction that would move your robot forward. This negates the need for the programmer to constantly recall that one motor is flipped.

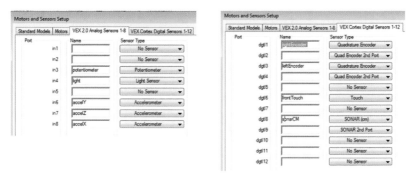

You can configure both analog and digital sensors in the Motors and Sensors Setup tool.

When I set up my sensors, I used three analog sensors: a potentiometer, a light sensor, and an accelerometer that measures along three axes, *x*, *y*, and *z*, each of which needs to be wired to an analog port if you're using that measurement. This means that if I were only measuring something along the *z* axis of rotation, I would only have to wire the *z* cable from the accelerometer. As far as the digital ports go, I used two quadrature encoders to read my motors. Each of these also requires two ports, but as you set the first one up, the second one is populated for you. The same thing is true of my ultrasonic range finder, which is listed as SONAR in the sensor setup page; I called this *sonarCM*. The ultrasonic range finder has an input and an output wire. The input must connect to the higher of two ports. Again, as with the encoders, the second port populates itself. Finally, I have one touch sensor on the front of my robot, which I will call the *frontTouch*.

Now that I've set up the motors and sensors, ROBOTC will automatically generate code for my robot. It looks a little like this:

```
#pragma config(I2C_Usage, I2C1, i2cSensors)
#pragma config(Sensor, in3, potentiometer,
        sensorPotentiometer)
#pragma config(Sensor, in4, light, sensorReflection)
#pragma config(Sensor, in6, accelY, sensorAccelerometer)
#pragma config(Sensor, in7, accelZ, sensorAccelerometer)
#pragma config(Sensor, in8, accelX, sensorAccelerometer)
#pragma config(Sensor, dgtl1, rightEncoder,
        sensorQuadEncoder)
#pragma config(Sensor, dgtl3, leftEncoder,
        sensorQuadEncoder)
#pragma config(Sensor, dgtl6, frontTouch, sensorTouch)
#pragma config(Sensor, dgtl8, sonarCM, sensorSONAR_cm)
#pragma config(Sensor, I2C_1,  ,
        sensorQuadEncoderOnI2CPort)
#pragma config(Sensor, I2C_2,  ,
        sensorQuadEncoderOnI2CPort)
#pragma config(Sensor, I2C_3,  ,
        sensorQuadEncoderOnI2CPort)
#pragma config(Motor, port2, rightMotor, tmotorVex393_
        MC29, PIDControl, reversed, driveRight,
        encoderPort, I2C_1)
#pragma config(Motor, port3, leftMotor, tmotorVex393_MC29,
        PIDControl, driveLeft, encoderPort, I2C_2)
#pragma config(Motor, port6, armMotor,
        tmotorServoStandard, openLoop)
//*!!Code automatically generated by 'ROBOTC'
configuration wizard !!*//
```

If I had to generate that much code from memory, and if I knew an error of even one character would mean the computer would not recognize the peripheral I had attached, I might go a bit bonkers. I think it is much better to use the setup configuration to automatically generate that code, don't you?

Now that we've gone through the process of generating all that code, I am definitely going to use it. For the remainder of this chapter, assume the robot I am referring to is configured with the sensors and motors as shown, unless I tell you otherwise.

Applied Math

If you're reading this book, I am going to assume you understand the basics of programming robots. If not, there are many great books in this series that can help acquaint you with the fundamentals. This book will start by covering some advanced topics (though not the most advanced by far). I will first show you how to keep your robot driving straight in relation to a wall. We will use an ultrasonic range finder to find our distance from the wall, and then, as we drive forward, we are going to correct our direction. Picture our robot with the ultrasonic range finder on the right-hand side, pointing at the wall we want to follow at a fixed distance. First we need to choose a fixed distance for our robot to stay from the wall. Let's say 10 centimeters (4 inches). The simplest way to accomplish this would be to check where the robot is. If it is too far from the wall, turn toward the wall; if it is too close to the wall, then turn away from it. However, we are going to add a twist to this basic zigzagging method of slow forward progress.

We will use something called **PID** to help our robot maintain a consistent distance from the wall and to drive smoothly as it progresses forward. PID stands for "proportional integral derivative." It is a standard feedback mechanism quite prevalent in most industrial systems. The basics of PID are identifying a target (in our case 10 centimeters), measuring your distance from the target (called your **error**), and correcting that error proportionally. So the farther away you get from your target distance, the greater the **correction** is going to be. This process continues in a loop until you signal it to end. By looping, the process continually corrects itself, with the idea that you will minimize your error because each time you are applying a correction that is proportional to your error. Let's take a look at how this would work within a program:

```
task main()
{
        int speed; // This line initializes a variable called speed
        int sonar_value; // This variable will provide the current
                reading of the ultrasonic range finder
        int distance = 10; // This line initializes a variable called
                distance and defines it as 10 centimeters
        while  (SensorValue (frontTouch) == 0)
        {
                sonar_value = SensorValue (sonarCM) // Store
                        the current reading from the ultrasonic
                        range finder to 'sonar_value'
                speed = (distance – sonar_value) *2   // Set our
                        current correction called "gain"
                if (sonar_value < 10) // If we are getting too
                        close to the wall
                {
```

```
                setMotor (rightMotor, 50 + speed); // Apply our
                    correction to the right motor
                setMotor (leftMotor, 50); // Keep our left motor
                    speed at 50
                }
                else // If our distance is greater than 10
            {
            setMotor (rightMotor, 50); // Set the right motor to 50
            setMotor  (leftMotor, 50 + (speed * –1)); // Apply our
                correction to the left motor
            }
    }
}
```

The first three lines of this program, those that start with
int, are telling the program to initialize a variable. I am using
three variables in this program: *speed, sonar_value,* and *distance.*
When you initialize a variable, you can give it any name you
want; it has no value or meaning until you define it later in the
program. I am going to use *distance* as my target. This is the
amount of centimeters I want my robot to be away from the
wall. And if you look closely, you will see that I defined this
variable as 10 in the same line in which I initialized it. The
other two variables will not be defined until after the program
starts because their value will be dependent upon other factors
in the program.

Though our program has started, the robot will do nothing
until it enters the loop created by the *while* command. The *while*
command is used to start a loop going that will continue as long
as a condition is met. In this case, I used the touch sensor. The

touch sensor can only return two states to the Cortex: pushed in, which is a 1, and not pushed in, which is 0. So basically I have programmed the robot to continue doing what I am about to tell it to do until the touch sensor is pushed in. This is ostensibly because I am imagining a wall at the end that it will bump into to stop. There is also a practical reason, and that is because if your robot is doing wacky things, you can always stop it by pressing the touch sensor. It's a little fail-safe I like to include in my programs.

Once the robot has entered the loop, it has some calculations to do and decisions to make. First it will define the variable *sonar_value* to be whatever the current reading of the ultrasonic range finder is. This value will constantly change as the robot continues through the PID loop, and that is the idea as we want to minimize error and eventually maintain a constant 10 centimeters away from the wall. The next variable, *speed*, is calculated by taking our target 10 centimeters as defined by the variable *distance* and subtracting our current reading (*sonar_value*) from that, then multiplying by 2. The amount we are away from the target distance is called our error. I want to make a correction in my program, so I multiply this error by 2; this is called the **gain**. The gain is the amount that I am going to correct my error by, and it is chosen through trial and error. There is no formula that says it has to be 2 in this situation. It was just a number I chose because I felt like it would provide enough of a correction to get my robot back on track. Remember, the goal of a PID is to minimize error by providing constant feedback.

Imagine if our ultrasonic range finder said we were 5 centimeters (2 inches) away from the wall. That would mean we are off our target by 50 percent. The error would be 10 − 5 = 5. If we multiply that 5 by our gain (2), we get our correction, which in this case would be 10. Let's now take a look at how we would apply that correction. I used an *if/else* statement to denote two conditions; one condition is if the robot is too close to the wall, and the other is if it is too far away. If it is too close, I have my left motor drive at a speed of 50, but I have my right motor drive at 50 plus my correction of 10, or 60. This means my right motor is going to go faster than my left motor, which will turn me to the left, or away from the wall, which is what I wanted in the first place.

But I won't get that far as the loop will instantaneously repeat. The controller will check my distance from the wall again and realize I am a bit farther away than last time, and I will therefore have a smaller correction to make. This correction will continue until I reach my target of 10 centimeters. The correction works in the other direction, too. Let's say I am too far away from the wall, 20 centimeters (8 inches). The controller will read that information, subtract the *sonar_value* from my target *distance*, in this case 10 − 20, or −10. It will then multiply this by our gain of 2 for a correction of −20.

The second part of our *if/else* statement addresses the condition of being too far away from the wall. I knew the value of the *speed* variable would be negative in this case, so when I applied the correction to the left motor, I multiplied it by −1 before adding it to 50. Meanwhile, the right motor is set to go at a speed of 50. In the example I just gave, the robot was 20 centimeters away from the wall, so I needed a bigger correction than the previous example. Let's go through the math: 10 (distance) − 20 (sonar_value) × 2 (gain) gives us a correction of −20. Multiply that by −1 and add the result to 50 and the left motor will drive at a speed of 70, significantly faster than the 50 of the right motor. But remember, it won't do this for long; as soon as it gets closer to the wall, the error will be less, so the correction applied will be less. This process should repeat until there is almost no error and the program is stopped when the bump sensor hits an object in front of it.

This next challenge combines the use of variables with some classic geometry. Variables can be used to help us count in programming. Often you want your robot to tell you how many times a particular event has occurred. For example, I will place a random number of strips of black electrical tape across one of the white tables in my classroom. I will tell my students to have the robot drive across the table and tell me how many pieces of electrical tape there are. Can you figure out how to program this?

There are a few things you have to consider. First, if you have ever tried to have a robot stop on a certain line (not the first) in a series of lines on a table, where the distinguishing feature of the lines is the difference in brightness of the line to the table, you may find that your robot got stopped on the first line and wouldn't move. My students often think their program is broken or they just get "stuck" at this point. What is actually happening is really quite revealing of robot behavior. The robot is still looking for the second and third and whatever number line you wanted it to stop on. But if you put the behavior (look for a line) in a loop set to repeat the same number of times as the line you're looking for, then you've hit on a classic mistake. The robot doesn't know lines, it only knows darkness or light.

If it sees a dark line and you've asked it to look for a dark line, it will repeat the loop and instantaneously see the same dark line and it will do it again and again, as many times as you told the program to loop. There are many solutions to this problem, but the simplest is to make each **iteration** look for dark, then light. By doing this, the robot moves forward off the line, looking for the bright table, before it looks for the next darkness (line).

Remember that in our challenge we are trying to calculate the number of lines in a given area. Let's say the table is 5 feet (1.5 meters) long. We have quadrature encoders on our wheels, so it won't be a problem to make our robot drive 5 feet, right? Right. We simply need to apply some basic geometry to our situation. First we need to understand that the **circumference** around our wheel is equal to the distance our robot will travel in one rotation of that wheel.

To make this work for us, we need to know how to calculate circumference. This is a pretty simple formula that I am sure you have learned at some point. Circumference is equal to the diameter × **pi**. Pi is a constant that represents the ratio of a circle's circumference to its diameter. Some very smart Greek mathematicians calculated its value thousands of years ago. In

IN STRAIGHT LINES

To see proof of the distance traveled in one turn of a wheel, take a piece of string and wrap it around the outside of your robot's wheel. That is the circumference (distance around a circle). Now take that string and lay it out straight. That is the distance the robot will drive in one rotation of that wheel. You've simply taken the circumference and stretched it out straight.

most modern applications, we use an approximation of pi as 3.14. So if you can measure your wheel's diameter (the distance across the center) and multiply that by pi, or 3.14, you will then know the circumference, or the distance your robot will travel in one rotation.

Are you still with me? Let's apply what we have so far. The table is 5 feet long and the diameter of your wheel is 2 inches (5 centimeters). You first calculate the wheel's circumference (C) using $C = \text{pi} \times D$, where D is diameter. Plugging our known numbers into this equation, we get $C = 3.14 \times 2$, which equals 6.28 inches (16 cm). My table is 5 feet long, so I am going to convert that to inches by multiplying by 12 to get 60.

The final step before we write our program is to divide my overall distance by my single rotation distance: 60 inches divided by 6.28 gives me 9.55 rotations. In other words, it will take my wheels 9.55 rotations to move my robot from one end of the table to the other. Because I don't want my robot to fall off, I am going to use a round 9 rotations in my programming.

Before I generate my ROBOTC code, I am going to use some pseudo-code to help clarify my thinking. Pseudo-code is a way of writing out your program in simple steps without resorting to the syntax that specific programming languages require. Here's my pseudo-code for this challenge:

1. Name a variable *count*
2. Set the variable *count* to zero
3. Start a loop that will end after nine rotations
4. Drive forward slowly
5. Wait for black (dark)
6. Wait for white (bright)

7. Add 1 to *count*

8. Continue until the loop ends.

9. Stop motors

10. Display the count on the LCD screen

For this program, we will assume I have added a light sensor and an LCD display screen to my robot.

Here's what the code in ROBOTC would look like:

```
task main ()
{
int count = 0 ;
        while (SensorValue (leftWheelEncoder) <9*360)
        {
        setMotor (leftMotor, 35) ;
        setMotor (rightMotor, 35) ;
        waitUntil (lineTracker) > 4000 ;
        waitUntil (lineTracker) < 500 ;
        count = count +1 ;
        }
        {
        setMotor (rightMotor, 0) ;
        setMotor (leftMotor, 0) ;
        displayLCDScreen (0, 0, count) ;
        }
}
```

The code pretty much follows my pseudo-code. I set the variable to 0 then started a *while* loop that was set to repeat while the encoder on my left wheel read less than 9 × 360. The reason for this math is the quadrature encoders read in degrees, 360 to one rotation. I then programmed my motors to run slowly while I waited for dark then light, after which I would add one to my count variable. The line trackers return values between 0 and 4,095, 0 for total light and 4,095 for total darkness. I chose some numbers close to these extremes, but far enough away to account for variances. Finally, when the loop is exited, my count variable appears on the LCD display screen.

The next example uses math to figure out the numbers to include in a program without addressing the programming itself as it's really quite simple, but getting there is hard. This is a project I do with my classes called the Wave. It was invented by Damien Kee and is used quite extensively in classrooms around the world. I describe the Wave as an interactive robotics dance. Identical robots are lined up next to each other, all facing in the same direction. Upon the start signal, they all move forward into a wedge shape, with the centermost robot driving the farthest and each pair of robots equidistant to the right and left of the center robot driving a little less. After they reach their apex, the center robot drives back, and when it reaches the next two, they start back with it, and then the next pair, and on until all robots are back at the starting line.

The next move the robots do is a split, in which every other robot goes in the same direction, for the same amount of time, then returns to the starting line. The final step is for each robot, starting at one end of the line, to go forward, backward, and forward, in succession, making what looks like a wave.

The tricky part for most students (if they're not the middle robot) is to figure out how long to wait for the others to come back. And this really stymies them. Some students start off by programming their robots to go forward for rotations or degrees. They quickly find out there is no easy way to calculate how many seconds one rotation takes. (There are ways to do this, but they are not readily apparent to a beginning robotics student.) However, most of my students are quite conversant with basic algebra, and so I break the moves down for them into a table and show them how they can apply algebra to figure out their wait times.

Let's imagine a class of eighteen students working in pairs, operating nine robots total. I am going to label these robots A through I. I'll put them in a chart for you.

Robot	A	B	C	D	E	F	G	H	I
Time Forward	1 sec.	2 sec.	3 sec.	4 sec.	5 sec.	4 sec.	3 sec.	2 sec.	1 sec.

You can imagine after executing this first maneuver, all the robots are arrayed in a shape like this:

The trick is to get each robot to wait for the one or ones in front of it to be level with it before it starts on its way back, too. To do this, we can call the time they went forward X. Then we use one example to illustrate how X will work. If we look at robots E, D, and F, we see that E is going forward for one second longer than D and F. Some students say that D and F have to wait one second then, but when you draw a line on the board going forward and backward they realize that they have to double that amount and wait two seconds for E to reach them before they start back. Armed with this knowledge, I then write the following equation for my students:

$$Wait\ Time = (5 - X)2$$

or spoken aloud, "Your wait time is equal to five minus X times two." Let's see how that looks in our chart.

	A	B	C	D	E	F	G	H	I
(X)Time Fwd.	1 sec.	2 sec.	3 sec.	4 sec.	5 sec.	4 sec.	3 sec.	2 sec.	1 sec.
Wait Time	$(5 - X)2$	$(5 - X)2$	$(5 - X)2$	$(5 - X)2$	$(5 - X)2$	$(5 - X)2$	$(5 - X)2$	$(5 - X)2$	$(5 - X)2$
Time Bckwd.	1 sec.	2 sec.	3 sec.	4 sec.	5 sec.	4 sec.	3 sec.	2 sec.	1 sec.

In the case of the center robot, we use an algebraic formula when it is not waiting at all because if it's a formula, it should work in every situation. So in this example, for robot E, $X = 5$, and $5 - 5 = 0$, and $0 \times 2 = 0$, so the wait time for the middle robot is zero seconds.

Math has a way of popping up when we least expect it. Robots and robot controllers have become so sophisticated that their inner workings are invisible to users. But we do have to program our controllers, and to write a program or figure out a problem in robotics, we are going to have to use some math.

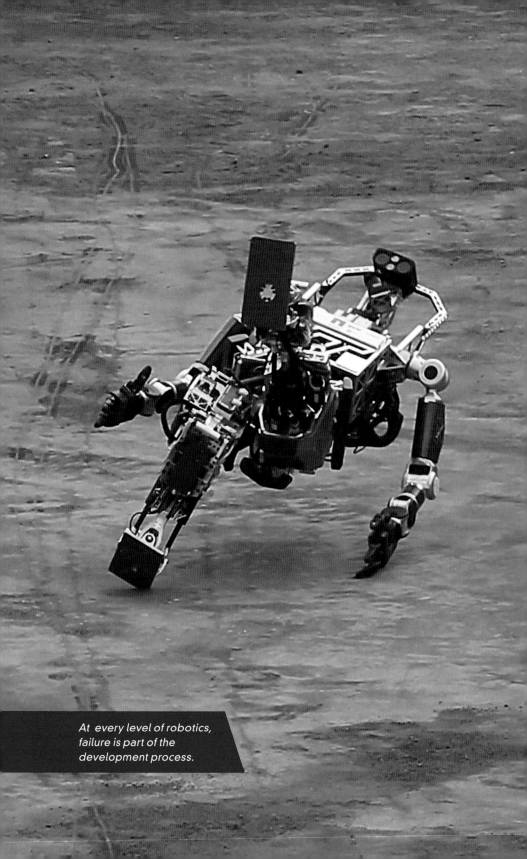

At every level of robotics, failure is part of the development process.

4 Everything Has Its Place

When you see your first robot, everything seems easy and cool. Someone will demonstrate a robot that does something cool, maybe navigate through a maze, shoot a ball in a basket, or pick up an object and place it somewhere. Or you might have attended a competition where robots are being driven around a field, people are yelling and cheering, everyone is wearing bright colors and costumes, and it looks like the whole world is having a grand time. You might even start building and programming your own, and pretty soon you have a little EV3 robot that can wiggle its way across the floor as it follows a line you programmed it to follow using a line-following program you found online. And then you decide to branch out and try your hand at something more complicated, something that there isn't a template for how to build or how to program. And the world falls apart.

Don't worry, you're not alone. This is a common occurrence. As a matter of fact, I would say it is almost universal. Whatever level your knowledge and skill in robotics is, there is always a lot of failure and many iterations of your project before it becomes successful. It's not enough to become successful in one case and think all of your troubles are going to go away, either. I still make the most common mistakes when I am building robots, even the ones I tell my students and teams to watch out for. Perhaps I make them a little less than before, but I still make them. And that's OK. If it wasn't a struggle, it wouldn't feel so good when you finally get your robot to be successful. At least once a trimester (and often times much more than that), I have a group of students stand up and jump for joy in my class. I ask them if they have ever done that in any of their other classes, and the answer is a resounding no. Not to denigrate other subjects—I am also a licensed social studies teacher—but it is those jumps and squeals of delight that make me know robotics is the right place for me.

By going through the troubleshooting tips in this chapter, you will not automatically build or program a better robot. What you will be able to do is recognize your mistakes more easily and rectify them. I am going to discuss troubleshooting categories in four areas. The first will be associated with placement of controllers and wiring, the second will be debugging programs, and the third—sprinkled throughout the chapter—will be common mistakes. The fourth area will be perhaps the hardest to work through, and that is teamwork.

Building the Robot

I am a big believer in form follows function. Simply put, this means that your robot must be built in a particular way to accomplish the function it was designed for. To build a robot purely with aesthetic considerations, or with aesthetic considerations first, is to invite failure. The coolest-looking robot will not be very popular if it does not work. For all of its cuteness, BB-8, the new, loveable **astromech** droid from *Star Wars: The Force Awakens*, would not be taken note of if it just sat there. If it didn't roll, make cute noises, shoot cables for stabilization, or have a lighter in its inner workings, then it would just be two orange balls, the smaller one on top. In this case, it was OK to build BB-8 to make cute noises; that's not aesthetics, or at least that's aesthetics following the function of being cute.

When my students build robots in class, one of the first things they go for is all the cool LEGO pieces: the colorful ones, the ones that look like claws or spikes, the ones that are animalistic in nature, and of course, the mini-figs. I allow all of this because personalization is important, and I am, after all, a teacher whose job is to get students interested in robotics. However, then I tell them that perhaps those things should

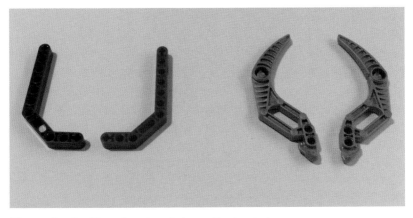

The coolest looking piece is not always the best piece.

be put on after they have designed the robot for its intended function. This compromise usually works best: build the robot to do what you want it to do, then make it look pretty.

Which of the sets of claws on page 65 looks cooler? Which set picks up objects better? I know the answer to the first question hands down: the grey ones on the right. I have proof of this in that I just ran into the kids' "LEGO Room" and found them attached together on one of their creations. The second question is much harder to answer. I would begin by asking, "What object?" "What is its shape and size?" "What about material? Will there be lots of friction or is it Teflon coated?" Then I would want to look at my existing robot to see which set of claws will fit together with the motors I have. Will I have to attach a new motor or move an existing one? After all of these considerations have been pondered, there still is only one way to answer for sure, and that is to try both. You really don't know until you try.

You may not have to build the entire robot with both sets of claws, though. You can more easily just take your controller, wire in one motor and build each attachment, testing them one at a time. For this reason, it is nice to have a spare controller (though obviously this is expensive and not within everyone's reach). But you can always prototype. Let's say you are building a robot for the VEX Robotics Competition. The pieces you are using are going to be from the VEX EDR system and will be controlled by the VEX Cortex. To build two gripper systems and try them out on your robot is time consuming. It also will frustrate the people who are working on the drivetrain of the robot, the programmers who are trying to test the robot for its autonomous capabilities, and the programmers who are testing its responsiveness during the driver-controlled part of the competition.

Instead of all fighting over one robot, find another controller. You may not have another Cortex, but you may have an EV3 or old NXT, and LEGO is often plentiful in robotics classrooms. You can simply prototype your arm out of whatever material you have available. It doesn't have to be fancy, and even if you don't have a motor to move your gripper, you can manually turn the gears. The idea is that there are other ways to test parts of your robot than just building a final version of everything and adding it to the robot to test.

Test, Don't Assume

I have digressed from the main topic of this section, and that is placement of controllers and wiring. But the two topics follow the same guidelines I have just laid down: form follows function. Prototype and test, and don't assume you know what will work. Compare different ideas.

When applying these rules to our controller, we need to keep a few considerations in mind. First and foremost is to protect the controller. The Prizm has a polycarbonate case which is nice, but it can still crack if hit with enough force. The Cortex is plastic and thin on the ends where it screws onto the robot. The Arduino is a circuit board without any sort of covering at all. So you want to protect these pieces by not putting them where they can be damaged. On the other hand, you want them to be accessible. I know of very few teams that wire their controller once and then leave it that way. Most teams will try a gamut of different motor and sensor configurations. Batteries must also be connected to the controller, and these are usually our bulkiest and heaviest items. So what do we need to watch out for?

A Faraday cage can block electromagnetic signals.

Swinging arms and other moving pieces are one of the main hazards to the controller. Place it so it is protected from these. If you shield your controller, do so with polycarbonate or some other type of hard plastic. My FTC team found out the hard way last year that surrounding your controller (in this case one of the Android phones) with too much metal creates what's called a **Faraday cage**. A Faraday cage is a metal box designed to shield an item from all electromagnetic interference. However, ours was not designed; it happened by default, and we inadvertently shielded the Wi-Fi radio signals being sent from one Android phone to another. Remember those students jumping for joy in my class? They were not the students on my team last season. Those had a lot of sad faces at our first competition. But we troubleshot our problem, fixed it, and then ran into a host of other issues involving wiring. Before we go on to wiring, let's finish the controller and battery placement.

Your battery will usually operate best toward the bottom of your robot, securely attached. We have found that during a six- or eight-match competition, our batteries run out of juice, so we always keep a charged 12V battery pack on hand.

If you have an electrical emergency—I'm referring to smoke and/or sparks emitting from your robot—it's always a good idea to have a master on/off switch. This is required in most competitions, but I suggest it for any robot that is using a controller with a separate battery pack (as opposed to an integrated system like the EV3 or VEX IQ). While you can disconnect the battery from the controller, it is often not easy to do, and you might even endanger yourself if you have to do it while there is bad stuff going on in your robot. But if you wire your battery to an on/off switch, then wire that switch to your controller, you have built yourself an extra safety mechanism and possibly saved your battery some juice by making it easy to

ZIP TIP

To swap out a run-down battery quickly, have a place to mount your battery and secure it with a zip tie. The process of zip-tying batteries, then cutting the zip ties and changing out batteries, may not be ideal, but it keeps them in place, and the switch time is usually pretty quick.

turn on and off. Some controllers have on/off switches, but if you protect your controller, it might not always be easy to access this switch. The emergency shutdown option is the way to go.

Some simple tools of the trade for eliminating electrical problems: a DC power switch, black matte electrical tape, heat shrink tubing in different colors, and velcro strips (really useful for attaching the phone). Don't forget to include some zip ties as well.

Wiring

Wiring, simply put, can be a nightmare. It can also be a beautiful thing when it is done well. There are a multitude of considerations when wiring a robot, but most of them boil down to this: you want your wires secure and your connections solid. That is much easier said than done. Let's take a look at securing wires first. To the greatest extent possible, you want your wires to lie flat and run along the robot to their destination. You don't want wires in midair if it can be avoided.

Sometimes it can't. The best way to do this is to run your wires through the **c-channel** or other aluminum pieces you have used to construct your chassis.

Wires being wires and having bendable metal inside the outer soft plastic wrapping, they tend to retain the shape they are bent to when you don't want them to, and they tend to bend the other way and lose their shape when you don't want them to. When possible, you want to secure your wires with a small zip tie. In order to save weight and provide attachment points, most aluminum building pieces for robots are machined with many holes. These are great because they allow you to securely zip-tie the wires to the frame. Not too tight though! A pinch and a break is a bad thing.

Our second consideration with wiring is solid connections. This poses problems with the new FTC competition rules, as all of the different controllers (servo, DC, sensor, etc.) have USB connections, and those connections are in the middle of the edge or back of each module. In other words, if the module is laying flat and the wire is running along the same flat surface, it will have to lift up a little bit to connect to the module. This place where it lifts is a very good spot for the wire to stress and slip out, or—as my team discovered—pull the USB mini connection

WIRING TIPS

When possible, you want your wires routed internally rather than sticking out over the edge of the robot, where they can be snagged or get caught on another robot. Keep your wires from bending at their connection points, especially at a 90-degree angle. Bends in wires should be gentle and not drastic.

loose inside the module and render it inoperable. This happened with my team where the OTG cable from the phone they used as the robot controller connected to the Core Distribution Power Module. Once the USB connection became loose, we could make a solid connection only in practice. As soon as we placed the robot on the field, the rigors of competition took over, and after a few seconds (usually about five), the robot lost the signal coming from the controller and died.

There are teams out there that have 3D-printed parts for their robots that have helped a great deal with cable management. And being the generous and helpful group of people that the robotics community is (and this is supported and encouraged by the competitions), the files for many of these parts are freely available to use and remix under **Creative Commons Attribution** licenses. Take a look at the one below:

A 3D-printed support for the USB cable to connect to the module and to keep the cable from coming loose

You have no idea how much my team wished it had used a part like this on its robot last year. The support wraps around the Core Servo Controller, and the screw holes match up with the ones on the module. Where the USB cable connects to the servo module, there are two extruded parts that will hold the cable securely in place.

Sometimes wires go so far as to snap off. This happens more often if you are connecting a piece with pins or socket pins (like VEX sensors and motors) than if you are using a modified plug-and-play cable. Of course, the tradeoff is the plug-and-play cable is most likely proprietary and is only going to work with a specific controller, where two-wire DC motors, three-wire servos, and three- or four-wire sensors are standard.

Before I conclude this section on wiring, let me take a detour to a potential troubleshooting solution for any potential issues you may face: the internet. There are forums for every competition out there. There are forums for every product out there. There are hundreds of thousands of people online offering advice and answers to questions for free and doing so gladly and happily. Take advantage. The answer to your problem is out there.

The picture on page 74 shows an example from a team that found answers to all their wiring questions. The only exposed wires in the FTC bot from the www.firstinspires.org website are toward the bottom, where the battery cables go toward the drive wheels. Even there, the wires are at least not sticking out. Everywhere else, the wires seem to be protected, wrapped, neatly tucked out of the way, and not bending at sharp angles. The controller (a LEGO NXT brick) and the emergency power

There is no wiring exposed on this robot to allow for a snag.

on/off switch are both placed on the top, where they are easily accessible. They are also securely attached to the robot.

Debugging

Debugging a program can be fun, interesting, or really frustrating. It all depends on how quickly you discover the bug and on how easy it is to fix the error. When we say "debugging," we are referring to finding errors in programs and fixing them. Sometimes the problems are glaringly easy to locate, but sometimes they are dastardly hard to find or to fix.

Though there are some common mistakes to look for in programs, we are going to be better served by learning how to write programs that minimize our mistakes and enable us to isolate errors quickly. To begin with, you should use proper file management. This is very difficult to teach to my younger students, and only marginally easier to teach my older students. Always name a program after what it does. While there is an undeniable tendency toward hyperbole when naming programs, "Killer_Death_Rabbit" does not convey as much information to another user as "Autonomous_FTC_Program2016." Nomenclature becomes important, especially when there are up to a dozen or more students or team members using the same robot and trying to experiment with different programs. To this end, we arrive at our second rule after proper naming of the program. Name each change numerically or with a date. If Autonomous_FTC_Program2016" is too long (and it feels that way), then try "AnFTCPro092116" for the program that was written on September 21, 2016. If it is changed the next day, someone can save it with "AnFTCPro092216." You are saving yourself a lot of angst if you have a chronological list of saved programs. Often a team will make tons of changes and additions, realize nothing works, then go back to the beginning, only to discover they can't find the last version of the program that worked, or they saved over that version and it's too late to go back.

Along with naming programs, there is also the need to comment on your code. I have read some snooty programmers state that if code is written well enough, they wouldn't need any comments because it would be clear what the code is meant to do. This is false, and arrogant to boot. Everything I have learned in programming is because people who comment extensively on their programs have allowed me to see how they work. This has enabled me to reverse engineer (work backward

WIRING WOES

Let's play a game and see how many trouble spots (and good points) you can catch in the way this robot was wired and put together. Take a look at the photo, and find your answers in the following list.

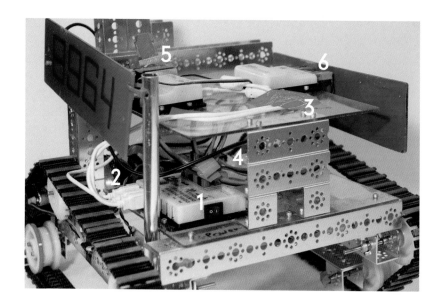

1. The Core Power Distribution Module is on a second inner level where it is protected, and the on/off switch is clearly reachable without any interference.

2. All three USB cables coming out of the Core Power Distribution Module are unsupported and bend quite radically (perhaps not 90 degrees, but not good). They also stick out from the robot, which is just asking for entanglement.

3. Those cables are taped down on the upper level so as not to loosen or get caught by stray robot arms.

4. There are several sets of Anderson Powerpole connectors coming out of the Core Distribution Power Module. It is nice that these are used, but they come in several different colors. I like to match colors on the ends of all connectors to make it easy to remember what motor goes where. It really can make your life easier.

5. We placed a DC drive motor toward the back left of the robot. Due to other build considerations, this motor was placed with the shaft pointing inward and the wires exposed toward the outside. Sometimes you balance some considerations with others. This is one of those cases, but that wire does look worrisome to me.

6. Finally, the DC motor wires coming out of the DC Motor Controller module on the top right seem to bend sharply where the purple team identification sign is pushing on them.

to see what the program does) their work and then see how it would be applicable to mine.

Most programming environments have the same standards for commenting on code. Anything written after two slashes is considered a comment and not part of the code. It looks like this: // and then the comment is written after.
In ROBOTC it would look like this:

```
task main ()
{
//the following code will spin my robot to the left for
        five seconds
setMotor (leftMotor, 67) ; //turn left motor on at half power
setMotor (rightMotor, –67) ; //turn right motor on at half
        power backward
wait (5000) ; //wait 5 seconds
stopAllMotors () ; //stop all motors
}
```

Did you notice all the mistakes I made above? Go ahead and read the comments and see if you can find any bugs in my code. I made two mistakes in the program above—one was intentional and the other I caught as I was going over it. The comments tell me I want to spin my robot to the left. But the code has my left motor going forward while my right motor is going backward. This would make my robot turn to the right, not the left. But since I have the comments right there, I can easily see what I wanted to do and I can isolate my mistake. The second error I made was with the wait time. I am used to using the *waitMSecs* command that has you wait for a given amount of milliseconds. So I wrote 5,000, which would be an inordinate amount of time in seconds for my robot to spin to the right (or left if I fix my other error). In this case, the correct command would have been:

```
wait (5) ;
```

Commenting on your code can be really useful, especially if you have a complex program. The more information you supply, the easier it will be to debug, improve, and add on to your code. And if you are working with multiple team members, comments can also serve as a communication tool among teammates. You can write down what you tried one day, what worked and what didn't work. That way, if you are absent, your teammates can pick right up where you left off by following your comments.

The next way to avoid the need for constant debugging is to collect snippets of code that work, save these, then use them as functions in a program. A function is any piece of defined code that can be used repeatedly. You can incorporate many lines of code into a one-line function. But before we create a function, let's talk about creating and saving code.

Let's say you have a robot base that is reliable and one you are going to use throughout your season. You want to be able to use this drive base for your upcoming competition. The competition hasn't been released yet, but from previous years you know that there will definitely be a need to turn at specific angles during the autonomous period. What you can do is create several programs. Title these "Turn45," "Turn90," "Turn180," and so forth. Then get to work on writing code for these programs.

Let's use the "Turn90" program, for example. Obviously this program will make your robot turn for 90 degrees. How can we do this accurately? There are a few different ways; I'll concentrate on one here that has worked for me.

When your robot is stationary, imagine the distance between the centers of your two drive wheels to be the radius of a circle. This is the circle we are going to travel parts of to work out our various angle programs. If our robot travels a quarter of the way around this circle, we will have turned 90 degrees; once I have established what it takes to travel ninety degrees, I can double that amount for 180 or halve it for 45 degrees.

When using this method, we have to have our robot make a pivot turn. A pivot turn means one wheel stays stationary while the other rotates; the robot pivots around the stationary wheel. The stationary wheel is the center of our imaginary circle, and the outside wheel will actually describe the circle as it travels around.

Time to plug in some numbers. Our robot measures 10 inches (25.4 cm) between the centers of the two drive wheels. That radius of 10 can be doubled to a diameter of 20 inches for our circle. Multiply the diameter times pi (3.14) and your product is 62.8 inches (159.5 cm). That is the circumference of the circle our outer wheel would keep going around if we did an indefinite pivot turn. We only want to go around a quarter of that turn (recall our eventual goal is to make a perfect 90-degree turn). So we divide our circumference (62.80) by 4 to get the distance traveled for a quarter of a turn: 15.7 inches (39.9 cm).

Hold that number in your head while we calculate the circumference of our wheel. Let's say our wheel has a 3-inch (7.6 cm) diameter; multiplied by pi, that gives us a circumference of 3 × 3.14 = 9.42 inches (23.9 cm). That is how far our outer wheel will travel in one rotation. Now we know the total distance we need to cover, 15.7 inches, and we know how far we travel in one rotation, 9.42 inches. By dividing our overall distance by our one-rotation distance, we can figure out how many times our outer wheel needs to rotate to make our robot turn 90 degrees: 15.7/9.42. Our answer is a repeating decimal which can be rounded to 1.67. So to make our robot turn 90 degrees, we need to have our outer wheel travel for 1.67 rotations. Easy enough.

```
task main ()
{
        while (SensorValue (rightEncoder) < 1.67 * 360)
        {setMotor, (rightMotor, 67) ;
        }
        stopMotor (rightMotor) ;
}
```

Though I always implore you to comment on your code, I have skipped doing so here because I am going to discuss the code right away. This program is simple enough. I set a *while* loop which waits for my encoder on my right motor to reach 1.67 times 360. The reason for the multiplication here is that the quadrature encoders count in degrees, whereas we deduced rotations in our calculations. The right motor will continue to turn at half power (67) until the encoder value is no longer less than 1.67 × 360. Then it will exit the loop, and the motor will stop; your robot will have made a 90-degree turn. Be sure to save this program as 90-degree turn.

With this little bit of code, we can start to create lots of programs and shortcuts that will save us from some (not all!) of our debugging problems later. For example, if we want to program a 45-degree turn, we just need to halve the number of rotations we used for the 90-degree turn. Our code would look very similar, with only one tiny difference.

```
task main ()
{
        while (SensorValue (rightEncoder) < 1.67/2 * 360)
        { setMotor, (rightMotor, 67) ;
        }
        stopMotor (rightMotor) ;
}
```

Instead of dividing 1.67 by two myself, I used the order of operations to create the equation and let the computer do the work for me. This is not only because I am lazy, but because it will remind me where the original number came from. If I plugged in 0.835, I might not know how I had arrived at that number.

Now that I have code for a 90-degree turn and a 45-five degree turn, and the knowledge to simply make other turns, I can create functions to help me reuse these "snippets of code" in other programs.

When creating functions, you first need to **declare** your function, which is a process of naming and defining it, then **calling** upon it later. In the scenario I am totally about to make up, my robot needs to drive straight for five seconds, turn left for 90 degrees, drive backward for three seconds, and finally turn left for 45 degrees, Here's the program:

```
7 void ninetydeglftturn ()
8 {
9        while (SensorValue (rightEncoder) < 1.67 * 360)
10       { setMotor, (rightMotor, 67) ;
11       }
12       stopMotor (rightMotor) ;
13 }
14 void fortyfivedeglftturn ()
15 {
16       while (SensorValue (rightEncoder) < 1.67/2 * 360)
17       { setMotor, (rightMotor, 67) ;
18       }
19       stopMotor (rightMotor) ;
20 }
21 task main ()
22 {
23
24       setMotor (leftMotor, 67) ;
25       setMotor (rightMotor, 67) ;
26       wait (5) ;
27       stopAllMotors  () ;
28       ninetydeglftturn () ;
29       setMotor (leftMotor, −67) ;
30       setMotor (rightMotor, −67) ;
31       wait (3) ;
32       fortyfivedeglftturn () ;
33 }
```

There is a lot going on in this program, so I have included the line numbers for easy reference. Remember, I would comment on each line of code if I were actually using this code. In lines 7 and 14, I have declared my functions using the *void* command. Once you have declared the function with the *void* command, you name the function by simply writing a name followed by open and closed parentheses. In the next line (8 and 15 in this example), you start the code for your function with a left curly brace, then include the commands for your function and finish it with a closed brace. The *task main () command* will denote that our actual program has begun. In the program, I drive forward at half power for five seconds, then stop (lines 24 through 27), then I call upon my first function simply by writing its name, *ninetydeglftturn* followed by parentheses and a semicolon. I then repeat similar behavior driving backward for three seconds and writing in my function for a 45-degree turn.

This use of functions in a small program may seem like a waste of time, but imagine if you had to program twenty-three 90-degree turns as your robot navigates its way through a maze. You could call upon the function twenty-three times or write the three lines of code that make that function twenty-three times for a total of sixty-nine lines of code.

TURNING TIP

You can include **parameters** in your functions that allow you to modify parts of your function. You can create a function that has a turn, but doesn't indicate the number my quadrature encoder is going to sense to stop the loop. You can supply that number each time so you will have one function that can be modified for turns of different angles. You can also make a parameter for speed, allowing for the use of negative numbers for a turn in the opposite direction.

The focus of our use of functions was to write cleaner programs that require less debugging. If your functions are accurate, then whenever you call upon that function, your robot should respond appropriately. But if you notice all your 45-degree turns are too slow, then you only need to check (and possibly change) the speed of that function once, and it will automatically change every time you call upon the function. This becomes extremely useful as you write complex programs.

When my students program their robots to drive in a square, they often watch as the first turn is a little off, the second turn is a little more, and so on. They will then begin to change the second or third turn amounts because they think this is where the problem is. What is actually happening is their robot is experiencing accumulated error. The first turn might be off by only a few degrees, let's say 3. Hardly a noticeable amount when you are making a 90-degree turn. But the second turn is going to off by 6 degrees, and so on. They won't notice the mistake until the third or fourth turn, so they will try to correct that behavior rather than adjust the first one. If they had used functions, and gotten the function as close to 90 degrees as possible, then there would be less accumulated error, and the robot would drive a more accurate square.

So far, all the methods we have looked at in this section are used to help us avoid having to debug. Eventually you will have to sit down and look at your code line by line to see where a mistake is. But if you have functions, commenting, and proper naming of program versions, it will make your job much easier. And sometimes the problem is actually related to syntax. This can be quite a bummer because there is a lot of syntax in the

C suite of languages, including ROBOTC. Luckily for us, ROBOTC has a **compiler** that will point out to us all the errors that won't allow the program to work properly. It won't let us know when we've made a wrong turn—it doesn't know what the humans want it to do—but it will let us know if you haven't written a command correctly to make it do any type of turn.

In the program where I taught you functions, I am going to take out semicolons in lines 8 and 17 and write one word wrong in line 27. When I do this, and hit the Compile Program button in ROBOTC, the result is frightening.

```
        File "C:\Users\RobotC\Desktop\Test2.c" compiled on Sep 19 2016 16:50:05
    7  ☒ **Error**:No body declared for procedure
    9  ☒ **Error**:Expected->'}'. Found 'while'
   11  ☒ **Error**:Executable statements not valid in 'main' declaration block
   12  ☒ **Error**:Executable statements not valid in 'main' declaration block
   13  ☒ **Error**:Unexpected '}' during parsing
   17  ☒ *Warning*:';' expected before '}'. Automatically inserted by compiler
   27  ☒ *Warning*:Undefined procedure 'stopAlMotors'. Global subroutine assumed.
```

That's all the errors we received by changing one letter and erasing two semicolons. Those red X's are fatal errors, and the program will not download to our robot with them. The yellow X's indicate errors that are not fatal but may not work on your robot. These errors can be annoying, yet usually they are helpful because they are pretty descriptive rather than just telling us there's a mistake and not what it is. For example, in line 27 it lets us know that *stopAlMotors* is an undefined procedure. Our program will still run with it, but nothing will happen at that point. The red X's are showing us where we have missed a semicolon, which may not seem like a lot, but a semicolon in ROBOTC defines an entire set of commands, and without it, those commands are useless.

Debugging is often a laborious process, but it is something every programmer needs to become conversant with. I haven't taught you how to sit down and check your code line by line because that is all you have to do. Sit down and check your code line by line. There is no substitute. But if you correctly name your programs, motors, and sensors, and you remember to comment on your code, utilize functions where possible, and use the Compile Program feature to correct your syntax, you will find that you have many fewer errors to debug.

Teamwork

There is no way to work around poor teamwork. In more than a decade of coaching robotics teams, I have come across all sorts of successful teams, and I have seen teams that suffer from very poor teamwork. The key to what makes good teamwork is rather elusive. I wish that after all these years I could make every team I have gel and work in beautiful harmony. I can't. What I can do is offer some tips to make teams work together better. These tips are not universal, and some of them may work better in different situations. It is up to you, the coach or teammate, to figure out what will work for your team.

The first factor to work on is establishing the goal of why the team is here. Presumably the goal is to win a robotics competition. You may have some students who say their goal is to learn or something else, but usually they are all about winning. Whether you win or not is immaterial. Having the goal is important. Winning as a goal is important because it allows you to focus on what is successful. It doesn't matter whose idea something was or who has the loudest voice or most forceful personality. Every decision can be assessed against the backdrop of what brings the team closer to the goal of winning.

For example, if you have two factions of your team arguing over which is the best robot design to accomplish a particular mission or score points on a particular obstacle, you don't have to argue the relative merits of each design—although you can. You don't have to choose the one whose designers can defend their choices most elegantly. You simply have to try out both designs and go with the one that is most successful.

Beyond this goal of winning, establishing team norms is another way to keep the team moving forward. A team norm can (and probably should) be as simple as making sure every team member gets a chance to be heard. All teenagers like to express themselves and be heard. They all have something to say. It's important to honor their voices and to seriously consider all ideas. Honestly, the iPod seemed like a crazy idea twenty years ago. Fifteen years ago, the idea of a smartphone seemed farfetched, at least as they exist now. No idea is too crazy to at least get a hearing, even if it's not acted upon. You can establish other team norms as you deem appropriate.

Team size is always a bugaboo. While at some point there is a maximum number that becomes too large to handle for any coach, I find that as long as you can find jobs to keep everybody busy, you are OK. The problems start when there are too many idle hands on a team. As long as there is something for everyone to do, you can handle a larger team size.

Teamwork is something that takes persistence and understanding. Sometimes you have to swallow your pride.

Make sure that each team member who is given a job is responsible for reporting back to the team. That way, the team members, the captain, and the coach are all able to tell who is pulling their weight and who may need some redirection.

Some of the people who are intensely into building and programming robots can be, uh, intense. One of the hardest things to let go of is your ego, especially in the heat of competition, when you're under pressure and you feel like you are the only one who can save the day. What you have to realize is most robotics competitions are designed so that you can't do it alone; you must work with the rest of your team in order to be successful. At this point, most competitions will penalize teams where one member is being bossy or not listening to the rest of the team. It is counterproductive to try to do it all by yourself.

FIRST LEGO League has a core value that I often return to season after season: "What we learn and discover is more important than what we win." I repeat this to my teams every year. Whether we make the state finals or bow out in early regional competitions, I truly believe my teams learn a lot either way, and that is, of course, the point.

Cameras on a drone need to work with a satellite network so they can send signals over long distances.

5 Distance Control

A lot of material has been covered in a short period of time in this book. We will start this final chapter with a review of the material we have covered, and I will show you how you can build on that material to further advance your knowledge and skills in robotics.

Controllers are the brains of robots, and this book has examined many different ones. At this point, you should be able to distinguish some of the main features of controllers. For example, are they plug-and-play controllers that automatically identify what type of sensors or motors you have plugged in, or are they a more general controller utilizing a standard wire protocol and ready to accept third-party sensors?

Knowledge not only of what the controller can do but how easy it is to work with will help you in deciding which one to choose. You may be comfortable with teaching yourself a new programming language like the Arduino Integrated Development Environment, using all the online resources and examples you can find yourself. Or you may just be starting and want to use an item like the EV3 that utilizes a graphical "drag-and-drop" programming environment that is easy to use while at the same time quite powerful. And you may fall somewhere in between those two, where ROBOTC, which has both a graphical and a text version, and works with EV3, VEX, and some Arduino boards, is just right for you. One of the best features about ROBOTC is you can convert your graphical program to text with a click of a button. Once you get comfortable with the syntax of ROBOTC, you may find that you enjoy programming more in the text-based version of the program, as I do.

Once you have chosen a controller to use, the next step is to build your robot and program. The focus of this book has not been building robots; see *Integrated Robotics* and *Advanced Programming and Design* if you are interested in learning more about how to build a robot. I did cover wiring of a robot quite a bit because that is the main connection to a controller that your sensors and motors will have. Other than making sure the controller is protected and not in the way of any moving parts on your robot (or other robots), you need to have it safely and securely wired.

If you have a controller and a robot, it is time to start programming. Programming is a never-ending endeavor as there is always more to learn: advanced commands and functions, new languages, and even quicker and more efficient ways of accomplishing a task. I have covered only a few programming examples in this book so far because I hope that by going in depth into these examples, you will be able to apply the lessons and methodology to other programming endeavors of your own. For example, if you know how to use a PID feedback loop to keep your robot parallel to the wall using a distance sensor, it is probably not much more difficult to figure out how to use a PID feedback loop to keep your robot at a fixed distance from a moving object or how to follow a line more smoothly than the traditional zigzag method most beginning roboticists use.

If you remember very little of the programming from this book but recall the lessons about debugging, you will do fine. If you recall, the majority of the information about debugging had to do with avoiding common errors before you make them. The more you train yourself to use good programming conventions like proper naming of programs, commenting on your code, and reusing sound code by creating functions, the better a programmer you will become. The rest is just practice and building knowledge.

So let's take some of the knowledge we already have and expand it. I am going to cover three new, extended topics in this chapter. First, we are going to learn how to attach third-party sensors to our VEX Cortex and make adjustments in our programs to make sure they are going to work properly. This will involve recalling our understanding of wires and voltage as well as some new skills in using the debugging window in ROBOTC to read our sensors and motors.

I will follow that with an in-depth look at how to connect two EV3 robots via Bluetooth and how to write a simple program where one can control the other. Then I will show you how to write a program that turns one brick into a remote-controlled device that can be used to control a BattleBot as it fights its way across your office, classroom, or kitchen floor. Finally, we will take a short detour into the world of cameras and learn how to attach one to your robot so you can locate it and see what it is "seeing," even when it is out of your sight. Let's begin.

Third-Party Products with the Cortex

You will recall the VEX Cortex uses a three-wire protocol for its analog and digital sensor ports as well as for most of its motor ports. It does reserve two motor ports for two-wire motors. These motors are powerful, but they are limited in that they don't have a third data wire to determine their position and stop them like you can with true servo motors. The two-wire motors can be used with the three-wire motor ports, however. They just need to be connected to a device called a motor controller, which is manufactured by VEX. The controller provides the missing data transfer that allows the control of the two-wire motor.

The two wires of the VEX 269 and 393 motors are for positive current and ground. This confused me at first as I always thought that a circuit had to have electrical current traveling in a loop and this is what made a circuit—the movement of electricity down one wire and back up the other. So why was I constantly seeing the terms "power" and "ground" instead of "positive" and "negative"? The answer to this question actually makes quite a lot of sense. Almost all DC motors (and all the motors covered or mentioned in this book) require positive power—in rare cases, some motors use negative power. So the wire (red) carrying the positive current is conveniently referred to as "power" (often with the voltage, as in 5V wire), and the other wire carrying the negative current needs a place to discharge, which is why this wire is called "ground." It has a connection to the earth, through the metal chassis of the robot body, so the current dissipates quickly and easily without shorting the system and, most importantly, without shocking you.

But what if you replaced a VEX 269 two-wire motor with a motor from a different company? For example, suppose I wanted to make a Fischertechnik motor work with my VEX Cortex. Could I?

Look at the wires in the image below. They're the same black and red wires on each motor. Those two colors are universally recognized; they are not chosen randomly. If you have ever jumped a battery in your car with a pair of jumper cables, you will probably recall that the end that attaches to the positive terminal on your battery is red, and the one that attaches to the negative is black. The black cable is supposed to be connected to any unpainted metal part of the car that is being jumped—this is grounding it, just like in a robot. The

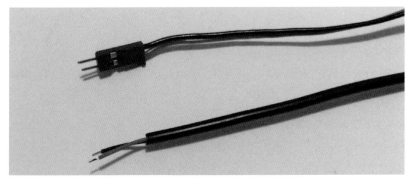

DC motor wires: VEX (top) and Fischertechnik (bottom)

next thing we would have to check is the operable voltage of this motor. The specifications on the Fischertechnik motor says it requires 9 volts, while the VEX 269 motor's operating range is 4.4 to 9.1 volts. Based on this information, I can assume that my Cortex will supply enough power to get either motor going. What about the wire itself?

The top wire on page 95 is the VEX motor wire, and the bottom is the Fischertechnik motor wire. VEX wraps its wires separately, while Fischertechnik wraps the wires separately, then puts that into a thicker black soft plastic tube. But what we're really concerned with is the ends. And these are exactly the same. Sticking out of the Fischertechnik wires are two exposed pieces of 22-gauge copper wire, exactly the same gauge (or near enough not to make a difference) as the VEX wires. The only difference is the VEX wire is in a housing with two pins connected to that housing and held in place via the exposed metal tabs you can see in the blue housing. These items are not hard to come by—but you probably will have to buy a pack of fifty or one hundred as they don't ship singles. A good supplier of these connectors and more is Hansen Hobbies.

The blue housing holds the wires and allows them to be connected to the pins that will insert into the Cortex. When purchasing, you're looking for a male futuba or JST or BEC connector. All of these are very similar products, and any of them should fit into the Cortex. Having a razor blade handy to carefully shave off a millimeter on one end or the other might be a good idea. The pins themselves are referred to as terminals, and you need to get ones that are compatible with the housing you purchased and the gauge of wire your motors are (probably

18-, 20-, or 22-gauge). And finally, you will need to purchase a crimping tool. It seems like no problem to use your thumb and forefinger or a pair of pliers to crimp a wire into a connector until you try it. You will waste a lot of energy and hurt your fingers making a mediocre connection. Splurge on a wire crimper.

And that's it. It may not make sense why you would want to go through all that to use a different motor with a VEX Cortex, but this is the advanced chapter. We are learning useful information to take our skills beyond what we already know. You may never use a Fischertechnik motor with a VEX Cortex, but extrapolate that knowledge for a second. Any two-wire DC motor that operates on DC voltage can be used with a controller—even one it was not originally manufactured for—providing you can make the connections work together. While some companies make their money by making a great controller and then making it difficult or impossible to use other products with their controller, the trend right now is for companies to make controllers that are compatible with the largest amount of products possible in the hopes of enticing people toward their products.

Let's now take a look at those sensors. I won't spend as much time on sensors as I did on motors because similar rules for connecting them will apply. We've already seen that VEX analog and digital sensors use a three-wire protocol. Red and black are again for positive current (power) and ground, while the white wire is for sending data. So any sensor that follows this protocol should be able to work. I have three peripherals from a company called PCS Edventures that I am going to connect to my VEX Cortex. The first is a red LED, the second is a digital touch sensor

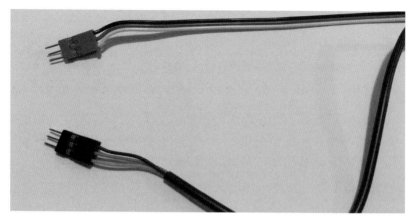

These sensor wires are made by VEX (top) *and PCS* (bottom).

(called a switch by PCS), and the last is an analog light sensor, which, as we'll see, will be the one requiring the most work.

Let's begin with the LED. As you can see in the picture above, the PCS sensors have an almost identical wire to the VEX sensors, except instead of white they have orange. While I could not find any PCS specifications, I am quite certain the orange wire does the same thing as our white VEX wire—it transfers data. So I'll go into ROBOTC and write a quick program to light an LED for five seconds.

```
#pragma config(Sensor, dgtl4, redLED, sensorDigitalOut)
//*!! Code automatically generated by 'ROBOTC'
configuration wizard


task main ()
{
SensorValue (redLED) = 1 ;
wait (5) ;
SensorValue (redLED) = 0;
}
```

This may be a bit confusing as the LED is not a sensor, but it is configured as a digital device. If it receives a digital signal being sent out, it will turn on. Remember, all digital sensors have only a limited number of values or conditions—for example, on or off, indicated by a 1 or a 0.

I can light an LED pretty easily. What happens if I want to use the PCS touch sensor? It is a digital sensor, so I am going to connect it to a digital port and write a simple program for it to work. I am going to write a program that will have the touch sensor turn on an LED.

```
#pragma config(Sensor, dgtl1, pcsTouch, sensorTouch)
#pragma config(Sensor, dgtl4, redLED, sensorDigitalOut)
//*!! Code automatically generated by 'ROBOTC'
configuration wizard

task main ()
{
waitUntil (SensorValue (pcsTouch) == 1) ;
SensorValue (redLED) = 1 ;
wait (5) ;
SensorValue (redLED) = 0;
}
```

This program worked to make the LED turn on for five seconds after I pushed in the PCS touch sensor.

It is an oversimplification to say that all electronic circuitry is the same because it is all based on digital ones and zeros. But that is a good place to start. And when it comes to spinning a motor, turning on an LED, or recognizing a touch sensor, the process is pretty simple, even when using non-VEX parts with a VEX controller. When you use an analog sensor, however, you are getting into slightly more tricky territory.

You'll recall an analog sensor returns a range of values as opposed to discreet numbers. The light sensor for VEX Cortex has a range of 0 (total brightness) to 4,095 (total darkness.) Whereas I know that a touch sensor is going to have two possible values, on or off, 1 or 0, I have no idea what values are going to be returned by a third-party light sensor. To test the new light sensor, I had to do two things. First, I wrote a simple program for the light sensor. This is actually a fake program. It waits for a certain value to be read by the light sensor and then will turn on the LED. Recall that I don't know what values my new third-party light sensor will show me. I don't even know if it will see dark as high numbers and light as low numbers like the VEX light sensor does. What this "fake" program will allow me to do is open up a tool called the Debugger Window.

The Debugger Window is an essential tool for learning what your motors and sensors are doing. In order to use it, you must write and run a program. You cannot just connect a sensor and open it up. However, once you run a program, you can open it and see what your sensor is seeing. You'll find it in the pull-down menu under the Robot tab in ROBOTC. There are many different Debugger windows you can look at: motors, sensors, variables, timers, joystick values, etc. You have to have downloaded your program and have your robot connected to the computer for it to work. Without both of these conditions, the Debugger Window will be grayed out and unusable. Here's what I saw when I ran the program, held the light sensor facing a white background, and opened the Debugger Window:

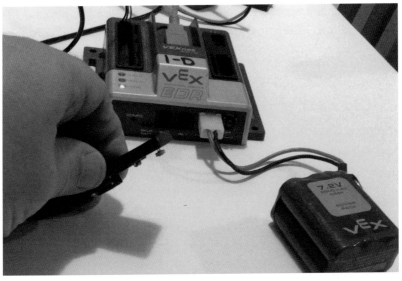

Sensors			
Index	Sensor	Type	Value
in1	pcsLight	Light Sensor	1921
dgtl1	redLED	Digital Out	0

Testing a PCS light sensor with the VEX Cortex

As it turns out, as I moved the light sensor around it returned higher values for brighter surfaces and lower numbers for darker surfaces. In this way, the PCS light sensor I used returned values in an opposite manner than the proprietary VEX light sensor does. This is why it is so important to use the Debugger Window, especially when using new sensors.

Bluetooth BattleBots with EV3

At the end of each term at school, the culminating project in my robotics class has been a SumoBot battle. Two robots are lined up in the center of a black circle, and when the round starts, they zoom back to the edge, sense a white line, then charge forward to try to smash each other out of the circle. My kids love it, and why not? Middle school, robots smashing, what else could you ask for? The only thing is, I saw a lack of sophistication in "smash, smash, smash!" I felt like there had to be a better way to find a final project that was as exciting but really challenged the students to use their robotics knowledge. That's when I hit on Bluetooth BattleBots.

I operate my BattleBots very similarly to SumoBots, with one important distinction: BattleBots are remotely controlled by a second EV3 brick using Bluetooth communication. There were several steps needed to create a remote-controlled BattleBot. The first, outlined on page 104, is learning how to pair two robots together. I will name one of them "Controller" and one "Responder." This helps me know which one will be sending signals and which one will be receiving signals.

Before we start with a remote control program, let's look at something simpler. Below is a program that allows me to click a button on one brick and have a second brick respond by making noise. The Bluetooth range of EV3 is pretty good as I can go outside the classroom door and do this from about 40 feet (12 meters) away. This usually impresses even the more jaded students.

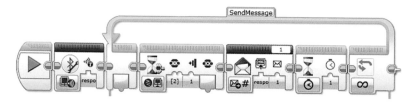

A simple Bluetooth send message program.

In this program, we first initialize a Bluetooth (BT) connection. You only have to do this on one program (send or receive), not both. And this will only work after you have paired two robots. After the BT initialization, a loop called SendMessage was created. Inside this loop, the robot waits for the center button on the EV3 brick to be pressed, and then sends a BT message. Below, I will look a bit more closely at this icon. After the message is sent, a one-second *wait for* is included (I place this to just slow them down; it is not absolutely necessary) and then the loop repeats.

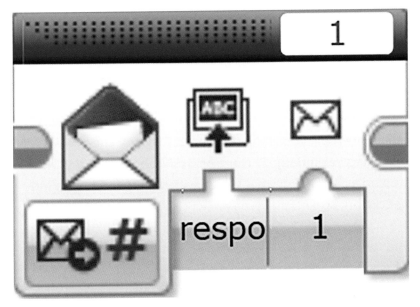

A close-up of the Send Message icon.

The picture above is the *send Message* icon. In the bottom left is where you configure what type of message you are sending. The forward arrow and number sign indicate that

GETTING CONNECTED

The pictures to the right are of my two personal EV3s, and they have been through a lot of abuse over the years. Here's the procedure for connecting them via Bluetooth:

On both robots (image 1), scroll across to the tools menu on the far right, scroll down, and choose *Bluetooth* (image 2). Make sure that the *iPhone, iPad, iPod* option is unchecked (image 3) as the robots will not see each other if you leave this checked. Now you can put one robot aside for a bit. It doesn't matter which one you use to make the connections; I usually use the one named Controller. On one robot, choose the *Bluetooth* option and scroll up to *Connections* (image 4). Choose this and then choose *Search* (image 5). It will take a while watching an hourglass spin around while the robot searches for other available Bluetooth devices. When it finds the robot you want to partner it with, choose that robot by scrolling to it and clicking it (image 6). A screen will pop up asking you if you want to connect. Click the check mark indicating yes (image 7). Now, on both robots, a screen will pop up asking if you want to pair with the other. Choose the checkmark again. Finally, a QWERTY keyboard will show on the screen asking for a passkey on both robots (image 8). The default key is 1234. I have never in my life changed this passkey. Now your robots are paired and will be able to communicate with each other wirelessly! You'll notice in the top-left corner of your robot that a carat < indicating Bluetooth was on will now have changed to a diamond <> indicating you are paired with another Bluetooth device.

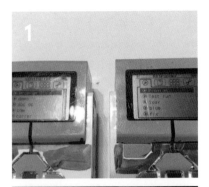

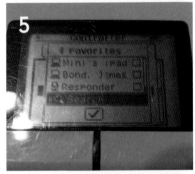

it is sending a numeric message. The "respo" is the name of the robot I am sending the message to; its full name is "Responder." Next to that is the message I am sending, in this case "1." In the top-right corner of the icon is the part that often confuses people. That is officially the message title. The confusion arises because I am sending the message "1" to mailbox "1" on the other robot. I tell my students that this can be thought of as the title of a book and the message itself as the content of that book. When you change the message title, you are telling the responding robot to look in a different book for a message.

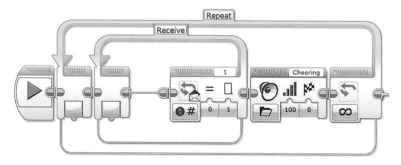

A simple Bluetooth receiving program

Above is the program for the responding robot. The program consists of two loops. Immediately inside the first loop is the second loop, which waits for a message. If you look closely, you will notice it is waiting for a numeric message in message title #1 to be equal to "1." If it receives this message (which it should if the center button on the controlling robot is pressed), then it will exit the loop and play the cheering sound at full volume. Then it will repeat and wait for the message again.

If you're still following me to this point, you should now try to make a motor move on one robot when a button is pushed on a different brick. If you can get this to work, then you're ready for the entire remote control program!

Moving Ahead

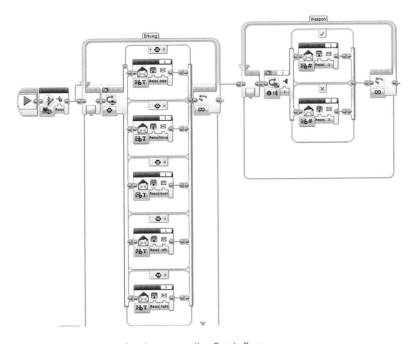

A Bluetooth program for the controller BattleBot

In this program for my controller, I have started off by initializing a Bluetooth connection between the two robots. Then I have two switches in loops. This is parallel programming, and though it is difficult to see, both loops are wired from the beginning of the program (after the BT initialization). These two loops will run at the same time. For ease of use, and because I have stressed in this book the use of proper nomenclature, I have named the first loop "Driving" and the second loop "Weapon." When I first ran this unit in my class, all my students clamored to have an extra motor run a weapon on their BattleBot. Who was I to argue?

I mentioned that this program uses a switch, and it does—it uses a rather large one. A switch is very similar to an *if/then* statement. In other words, if this happens, do that. In this switch, however, there are many different *ifs* that could happen. Look at the first orange icon inside the loop. It has a graphic of the buttons on top of the EV3 brick. This is a brick button switch. This means that depending on what button is pressed, the switch will go to a different command that corresponds to that button.

Start at the top. The buttons are all black in this image. That is because this is the condition for "No Button." This was essential for the program, otherwise the robots would continue some behaviors even when no button was being pushed. In this case, if no button is pushed on the controller brick, then the text message "stop" will be sent to mailbox 1 on the responding brick.

As you go down the list, you will start to recognize a pattern. If the top button is pushed, the message "forward" will be sent. If the bottom button is pushed, the message "reverse" is sent. And the right and left buttons follow the same pattern accordingly. And this switch is in a loop, so the robot will constantly send messages to the BattleBot.

The second switch in a loop is for the weapon, which was usually some sort of swinging hammer or smashing gate attached to a medium motor on the BattleBot. This switch is a little more reasonable. It has two conditions only: whether or not a touch sensor has been pushed in. If it has, a 1 is sent; if not, a 0 is sent. Notice the numbered messages are being sent to mailbox 2, while the text messages were being sent to mailbox 1.

That's it for the controller bot's program—just two switches. Based on which brick buttons are pushed and whether a touch sensor is pushed in, the BattleBot will drive around and swing a weapon. Let's see how the BattleBot has its program arranged to respond to these messages.

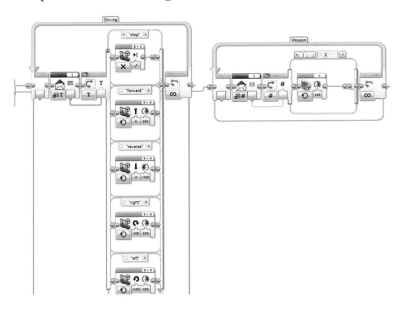

A Bluetooth program for the receiving BattleBot

This program very nicely mirrors the controller program. A loop is set up, and inside that loop a *receive message* block is placed. Notice it is receiving from mailbox 1, and it is configured to receive a text message. It then wires the contents of this text message into a switch. Depending on the contents of this message, the robot will drive forward, backward, spin left, or spin right.

The second loop is also wired into the beginning of the program so the weapon can operate at the same time as the BattleBot is driving around. This switch only had two possibilities: a 1 will make the medium motor in port A turn on at full power and a 0 will turn it off. You may notice that you cannot see the second switch condition below the first one in this example. That is because I used "tabbed view," which is a way of collapsing that long list so that each option is arranged in tabs that are stacked on top of each other. You have to scroll across to see them. Sometimes it's hard to remember what you have done when you're in tabbed view because you can't see, but

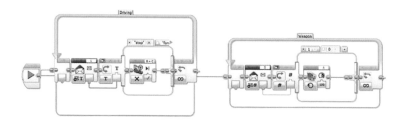

The receiving BattleBot program in tabbed view

on the other hand, it saves a lot of space:

Below is the same program, but a lot smaller. To find each condition, you just have to scroll from left to right. One final note on BattleBots: There are many different ways to move your bot about. You could have used a motor with a wheel attached to it. When you turn the wheel one way, your robot turns that way; when you turn it the other direction, the robot turns again. A touch sensor could be used for forward and backward. A motor again could be used to control speed. The above examples were just that, examples. Experiment and see what you can come up with on your own.

Adding Sight

The last idea I want to explore is that of attaching a camera to our robot. It seems like such a logical thing to do. Drones use them all the time for taking pictures and to allow operators to see where they're flying when the drone is out of view. Search-and-rescue robots use them so the operators can see what the robot is finding in the rubble of buildings. And of course, it is really cool to be able to see something that you can't physically capture with your own eye at the moment.

The first option I want to look at is the simplest, and it is not one in which a camera will send pictures directly to another device. This category is more accurately called "Image Sensors," and they act just like a sensor, which can send signals to your controller when it senses certain images. One of the popular models of an image sensor is the PixyCMU Cam5.

The PixyCam searches for images and can be taught to look for specific images (colors, shapes, etc.) and send information to the robot when those are found. It also is extremely versatile in that it connects over any of the following ports: UART serial, SPI, I2C, USB, or digital/analog output. Sound familiar? This allows it to be compatible not only with LEGO Mindstorms and NXT/EV3, but also with Arduino, Raspberry Pi, and other controllers.

So how do you see what Pixy is seeing? One way would be to have it use the Bluetooth capabilities we learned about. On one robot, you could write a program that uses a switch to display one of ten different images, depending on what message it is sent. On the robot with the PixyCam, you could have a program running that will look for images, and depending on which one it sees, it will send a message to the receiving robot, which can then scroll through its program and display the correct image.

Another way is to use PixyMon, an application (Windows, MacOS, Linux) that lets you see what Pixy is seeing. This capability is not wireless; you need to be connected to Pixy via a micro-USB cable. So what do we do if we want to be able to see what our robot's camera is seeing even when it is far away from us?

Another option you have is an app available for Android phones only called IP Webcam. This free app (there is, of course, a pro version you can pay for) allows you to stream any video from an Android phone onto a computer. You don't need an internet connection, but you do need a Wi-Fi network to connect your phone to your computer. The pros of a setup like this are you can use any Android phone, even an older one that you no longer want. You only need to mount it on your robot. You don't have to connect it to your controller, which is one less thing to worry about. The cons are you are limited to the distance that the Wi-Fi network you create with your computer can reach—this may be only as far as a few rooms over or down the hall and around the corner. And if you don't have an extra phone, you are risking your phone. Given these limitations, this would be a great option for a robotics competition where you want to get a robot's-eye view of the game. Just make sure the rules of the competition allow you to mount a camera.

We have a low-cost option for our EV3 or NXT in PixyCam, and we have a no-cost option with IP Webcam downloaded onto our Android phone. But what if you want a quality, dedicated camera that has Wi-Fi connectivity, good image processing, and reliability? Then you're going to pay for it. That doesn't mean you're going to break the bank, just that you're going to get what you pay for. Any Wi-Fi-enabled camera is going to cost more as you go for better or faster image processing. And you're also going to pay more for more powerful Wi-Fi capability. Finally, if you want a camera that can stream images from miles away, then you're going to need one that can work over a satellite network, and that is going to cost you.

The key to adding functionality to your robot like a camera is to remember not everything has to run through your controller. While sensors and motors have to be integrated, cameras may be one area where it is better to mount it on the robot but to run it using separate hardware and software.

Whether you're battling robots, fiddling with wires to add a whole bunch of third-party sensors to your robot, or mapping your office building with a camera mounted on your robot, I hope I have helped you with some ideas on how to proceed. I will never be able to address all concerns, situations, and possibilities in one book. Please use the resources in the back of this book for further exploration. And remember, there is no substitute for just sitting down with a robot and playing; that is the way most of us learned and how most of us still learn.

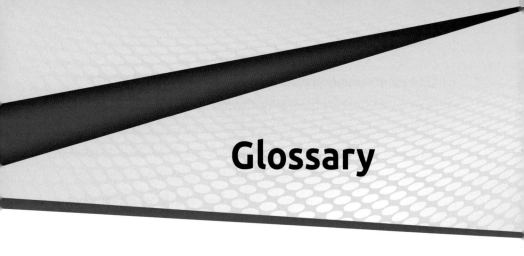

Glossary

analog sensor A sensor that returns a range of values.

Anderson Powerpole connectors A newer standard for connecting wires carrying DC power.

Android phone Any phone running the Android operating system, such as those used in the FTC competition.

Arduino A set of microcontrollers becoming quite popular in recent years.

astromech A class of droids in the Star Wars movie franchise designed to help with navigation of rebel fighter ships.

bits The smallest-sized piece of information sent by a computer, either a 0 or a 1.

Bluetooth A widely used wireless communication protocol.

breadboard A plastic-coated board full of socket pin holes with a conductive surface, used for prototyping electronics.

brick A common name for the controller in many robotics products, such as the EV3 brick.

BrickPi A robot produced by Dexter Industries that uses a shield connected to a Raspberry Pi and is capable of interfacing with all LEGO EV3 and NXT motors and sensors.

bus A communication device that allows many resources to talk to a computer or a controller.

byte A collection of eight bits.

cable A collection of wires bundled together in a soft plastic covering, usually with a phone jack–type of connector on the end.

call To activate a function by writing its name.

c-channel A long piece of aluminum or other metal that is shaped like a C; it allows for efficient placement of wires.

circumference The distance around a circle, such as a robot's wheel. It is equal to the distance the robot will travel in one rotation.

command Any single instruction given to a robot.

compiler Part of programming software that takes the program you have written and converts it into machine language readable by your robot.

controller The part of the robot that executes programs by taking information in from sensors, processing it, and sending commands out to motors and other output devices.

correction The mathematically derived change made to an action in a PID feedback loop.

Creative Commons Attribution A license that allows a user to reuse information found online, such as a robotics program, provided attribution is provided to the original author.

DC motor A motor that operates under direct current; without an encoder, it is difficult to stop DC motors after a particular amount of rotations.

debugging The process of going through a program line by line, looking for the mistake you may have made.

declare To name a function.

digital sensor A sensor that returns a discreet range of values.

distance sensor A sensor that uses sonar or some other type of wave to determine distance by timing how long the emitted wave takes to travel back to the robot.

DIY Abbreviation for "do it yourself"; in robotics, it refers to building a robot or part of a robot yourself, using pieces you purchased or built rather than those from a kit.

dongle Any device attached to a computer or robot that physically sticks out.

error The difference between the actual measured value and the target value in a PID feedback loop.

EV3 The current line of robotics solutions from LEGO Mindstorms Education.

Faraday cage A metal cage built to protect a device from electromagnetic interference.

FIRST For Inspiration and Recognition of Science and Technology; a robotics organization that runs a suite of competitions for students from kindergarten to twelfth grade.

FTC FIRST Tech Challenge; a robotics competition for middle and high school–aged students.

function A set of commands that have been combined into one and given a new name.

gain An amount that the error is multiplied by in order to arrive at the correction in a PID feedback loop.

graphical language Any programming language that uses graphical icons.

ground The wire that provides a connection to the earth and is separate from the traveling current in the other wire.

hardware Any physical part of a computer or robotics system.

H-bridge An electronic circuit that allows a DC motor to run back and forth.

iteration One complete occurrence of a repeating process or action.

I2C Inter-Integrated Circuit; a specialized port that allows the connection of a bus to a controller, allowing for communication with many devices.

LCD Liquid crystal display; a type of display used on screens in electronics instruments.

microcontroller A small controller on one circuit board with input and output sockets, a processor, and memory.

micro SD card A small secure disk that can hold a lot of information.

OTG cable On-the-go cable is designed to allow two-way communication between devices using USB.

parameters Changeable inputs you can assign to a function.

peripherals Any devices attached to a robot that are not germane to its functioning.

pi A mathematical constant that is the ratio of a circle's circumference to its diameter.

PID Proportional integral derivative is a type of feedback loop that calculates an error and corrects the actions of the system in proportion to the amount of that error, with the hope that it will lessen over time.

plug and play Any device that can be connected to a robot and work instantly without installing extra software or writing new drivers.

polycarbonate A hard type of plastic.

port Any opening on a controller that accepts a certain type of wire or cable.

processor The brain of a controller, where programs are executed and information is read.

proprietary Items that are made to work only with other items from the same manufacturer.

prototype A model of a robot or other structure, usually made out of less expensive and easier to use material than the final product; also, to make such a model.

PWM Pulse width modulation is a method of controlling speed in a DC motor without reducing strength.

quadrature encoders Sensors that can determine the position and direction of a DC motor.

radar A device that detects objects and their speed and direction using electromagnetic waves bounced off of objects and back to the device.

range-finding laser Laser beams deployed to detect objects at far distances.

Raspberry Pi A microcomputer that sits on one circuit board, has a processor and flash memory, and can connect to peripheral devices like a monitor, keyboard, etc.

SCL The clock line in an I2C bus; it provides the synchronization between the clocks on two devices so communication doesn't get garbled.

SDA The data line in an I2C bus, responsible for the transmission of data from the devices on the I2C bus and another device.

sensor Any device designed to measure and relay information about observable phenomena.

servo motor A motor that turns to a specific location; most servo motors turn between 0 and 90 or 180 degrees.

shield A device that connects to multiple points on a controller or microcomputer, transforming the capabilities of the original.

Smart Hub The name of the controller in the LEGO WEDO system.

software The programs and code that run machines and robots.

stall When a DC motor stops turning due to the power load (current) being less than the torque of the motor shaft.

text-based language A programming language that is written in text.

third-party Describing any peripheral designed by one company but compatible with parts produced by another company.

torque Turning power.

UART Universal asynchronous receiver/transmitter is a method of providing serial communication between two devices where the data rates are configurable.

ultrasonic range finder The name of the distance sensor designed by VEX for its Cortex.

USB Universal serial bus is the standard in data transfer wires in most electronic communication.

volts A unit of electronic potential.

wire A long piece of soft metal capable of conducting electricity and used to transmit power and data.

Further Information

Competition Websites

FIRST Robotics Competition

www.firstinspires.org

This site is the clearinghouse for all FIRST competitions from Jr. FLL to FRC. You can find rules, registration, and area event information here.

High Tech Kids

www.hightechkids.org

This site, run by volunteers in the state of Minnesota, provides free resources and training for teams competing in FLL and other competitions. It is the first site I went to over a decade ago when I started coaching FIRST LEGO League.

International Robot Olympiad

www.iroc.org

One of the most popular robotics competitions, IROC is for children from under the age of eight to college undergraduates.

Robotics Education and Competition Foundation

www.roboticseducation.org

The Robotics Education and Competition Foundation provides two separate competitions for VEX IQ and VEX EDR robots.

Instructional Websites

Carnegie Mellon Robotics Academy

education.rec.ri.cmu.edu

The Carnegie Mellon Robotics Academy home page provides links to resources for students and teachers for both VEX and LEGO formats.

Damien Kee's Technology in Education Page

www.damienkee.com

Damien Kee has been a leader in educational robotics for over a decade now. He has written several books on robotics, and his design for Riley Rover is used in hundreds of classrooms (including mine) around the world. I highly suggest you join his robotics email group (sign up from his site).

Ian Chow-Miller's YouTube Page

www.youtube.com/ianchowmiller

There are hundreds of videos on Ian Chow-Miller's YouTube page, many of which help illuminate a lot of the topics covered in this book.

LEGO Education Community

community.education.lego.com

LEGO Education has provided this community forum to help its users question, explore, share, and communicate their ideas with each other and with LEGO Education employees.

LEGO Engineering

www.legoengineering.com

Hosted by Tufts University Center for Engineering Education and Outreach (CEEO), this site contains hundreds of articles pertaining to the world of robotics education. The author of this book is a contributor.

LEGO MINDSTORMS Blog

www.thenxtstep.com

This blog didn't change its name when LEGO created the EV3 line, but it is very current with information related to the EV3 as well as other issues in robotics.

ROBOTC Forum

www.robotc.net/forums

If you have a question about ROBOTC, you can find the answer here. With thousands of members and quick, in-depth responses, this is a great site for receiving quality information.

STEM Robotics 101

stemrobotics.cs.pdx.edu/node/291

This site provides curriculum for robotics classes. The curriculum is free and customizable, and anyone with an account can add to it or mix different parts into their own.

Product Websites

AndyMark

www.andymark.com

AndyMark is a robotics parts supplier with many good options for motors, actuators, servos, etc. AndyMark is a sponsor of FIRST Robotics and supplies many of the items in the kit of parts.

Hansen Hobbies

www.hansenhobbies.com

Hansen Hobbies is a supplier of almost any electrical device or product you need.

LEGO Education

www.legoeducation.us

In the USA, this is the site for purchasing all LEGO Mindstorms robots and related products.

McMaster-Carr

www.mcmaster.com

McMaster-Carr is a huge supplier of all things fabrication and manufacturing. This site is good for looking up off-the-shelf odds and ends or even for purchasing raw materials.

RobotShop

www.robotshop.com

This online shop can provide you with parts for your robot or with some of the latest high-tech toys.

Tetrix Robotics

www.tetrixrobotics.com

Tetrix Max and Tetrix Prime are two of the main building platforms for FTC robots. With the addition of the Tetrix Prizm to their product line, they look to be an important company in high school robotics.

VEX Robotics

www.vexrobotics.com

This is the site to purchase all VEX Robotics materials including the EDR and IQ lines.

Index

proprietary, 15, 17, 19, 21, 27–28, 73, 101

prototype, 20, 41, 66–67

PWM, 25–26, 33, 39

quadrature encoders, 38–40, 48, **48, 49**, 56, 58–59, 81, 84

radar, 6

range-finding laser, 6

Raspberry Pi, 11, 32, 36, 112

remote control, 8–10, 13, 22–23, 44, 93, 102–104, **102, 103, 105**, 106–111, **106, 107, 109, 110**

ROBOTC, 29, 45–49, **47, 48, 49**, **51–52**, 52–55, 58–59, **58**, 78–79, **78**, 81–84, **81, 82, 83**, 86, **86**, 92–93, 98–100, **98**, **99, 101**

SCL, 27–28

SDA, 27

servo motor, 21, 31, 39, 43, 47, **47**, 71, 73, 94

shield, 11, 32, 36, 40

Smart Hub, 17–19, **18**, 41

software, 6, 10, 20, 22, 28–30, 33, 40–41, 45, 113

stall, 25

text-based language, 11, 45, 92

third-party, 21–23, 27–29, 39, 46, 91, 93–101, **95, 98, 101**, 113

torque, 25

UART, 26, 28–29, 111

ultrasonic range finder, 30, 48, **48, 49**, 50, **51**, 53

USB, 9–10, 21, 32–33, 38, 42–44, 71–73, **72**, 76, 111–112

VEX EDR, 11, 23–24, **24**, 26–30, **30**, 41, 45–46, 53, 66–67, 93–97, 100, **101**

VEX IQ, 10, 20–23, 28, 35, 45, 69

volts, 25–29, 38–39, 41, 69, 95–96

wire, 10–11, 24–31, **24**, 37–40, 42–43, **43**, 48, 64, 66–67, 69–73, **74**, 76–77, **76**, 91–98, **95, 98**

About the Author

Ian Chow-Miller is a New York native who has lived in Tacoma, Washington, for the past nine years. He began his career as a social studies teacher but switched to robotics more than a decade ago and hasn't looked back. He has written curriculum for robotics and trained teachers around the country. He is a member of the LEGO Educator's Advisory Panel and is a constant contributor to Tufts University's LEGO Engineering website. Ian has coached FIRST LEGO League consistently since 2004, and when robotics season ends, he starts coaching soccer. He is married to an awesome wife and has two great sons who are budding engineers.